JOE BONAMASSA ROYAL TEA

AUTHENTIC TRANSCRIPTIONS
WITH NOTES AND TABLATURE

Music transcriptions by Pete Billmann,
Jeff Jacobson and Paul Pappas

ISBN 978-1-7051-2030-9

DOWNTOWN
MUSIC PUBLISHING

EXCLUSIVELY DISTRIBUTED BY

Visit Hal Leonard Online at
www.halleonard.com

Contact us:
Hal Leonard
7777 West Bluemound Road
Milwaukee, WI 53213
Email: info@halleonard.com

In Europe, contact:
Hal Leonard Europe Limited
42 Wigmore Street
Marylebone, London, W1U 2RN
Email: info@halleonardeurope.com

In Australia, contact:
Hal Leonard Australia Pty. Ltd.
4 Lentara Court
Cheltenham, Victoria, 3192 Australia
Email: info@halleonard.com.au

When One Door Opens

Words and Music by Joe Bonamassa, Peter Brown and Kevin Shirley

Drop D tuning:
(low to high) D-A-D-G-B-E

Intro

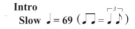

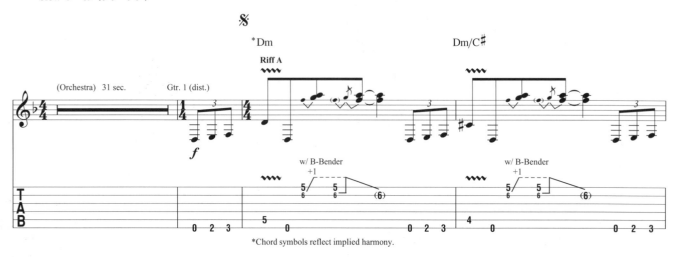

*Chord symbols reflect implied harmony.

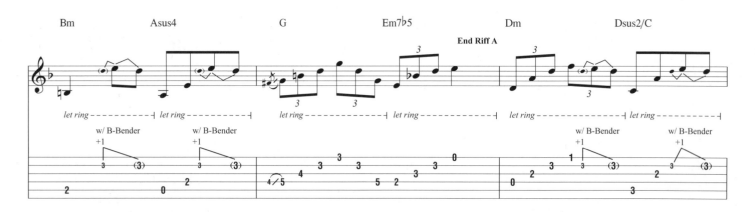

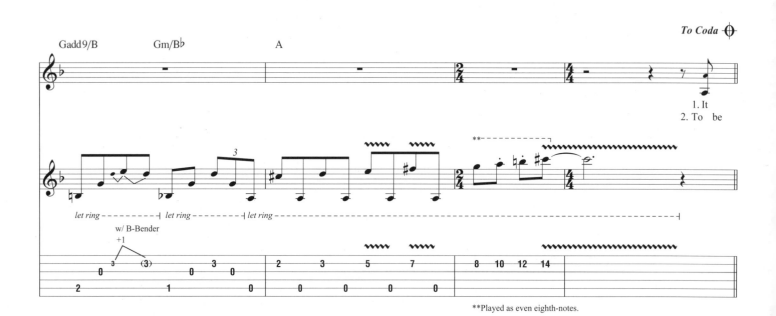

**Played as even eighth-notes.

Verse

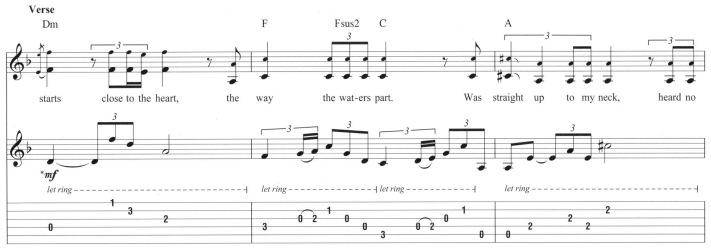

starts   close to the heart,   the way   the wat-ers part.   Was   straight   up   to   my neck,   heard no

*Control dynamics w/ vol. knob throughout.

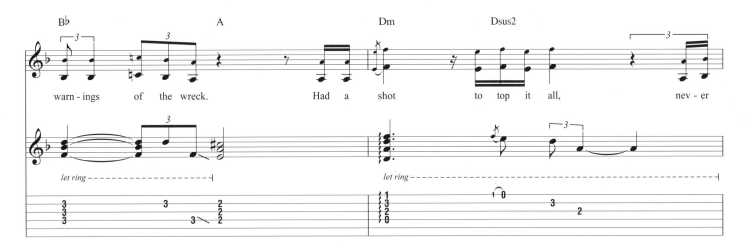

warn-ings   of   the wreck.   Had   a   shot   to top it all,   nev - er

feared   the fall.   A   life - time   of   gold,   hope it   lasts un - til I'm old. __   Are you a

Chorus

ty - coon   or a Mo -   ses.   Do you   see __   what __   light   ex - pos - es. __   Ev - 'ry

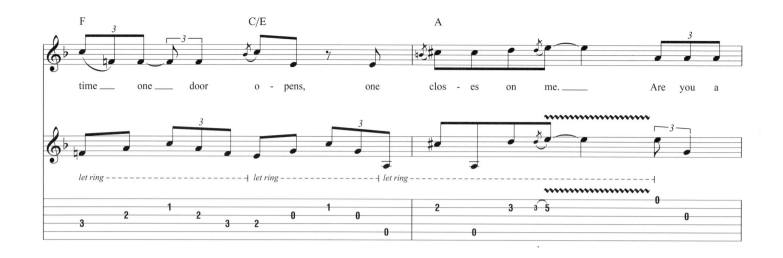

time ___ one ___ door o - pens, one clos - es on me. ___ Are you a

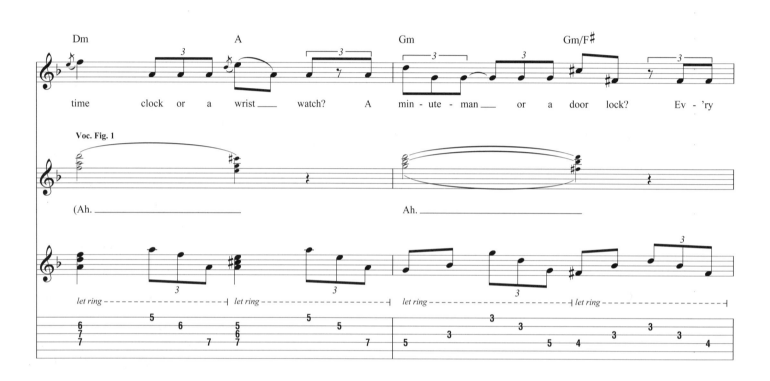

time clock or a wrist ___ watch? A min - ute - man ___ or a door lock? Ev - 'ry

Voc. Fig. 1

(Ah. _____ Ah. _____

D.S. al Coda

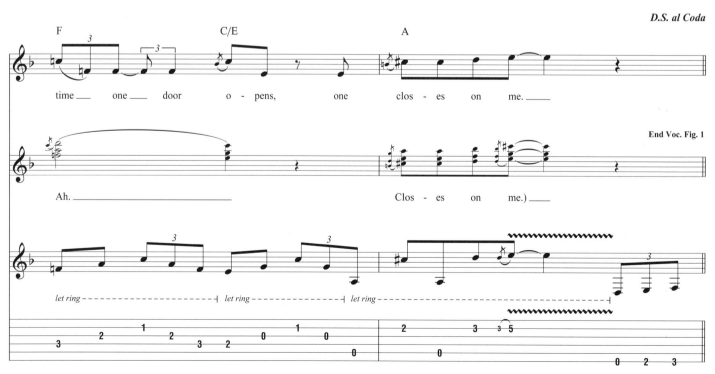

time ___ one ___ door o - pens, one clos - es on me. ___

End Voc. Fig. 1

Ah. _____ Clos - es on me.) ___

⊕ Coda

Verse

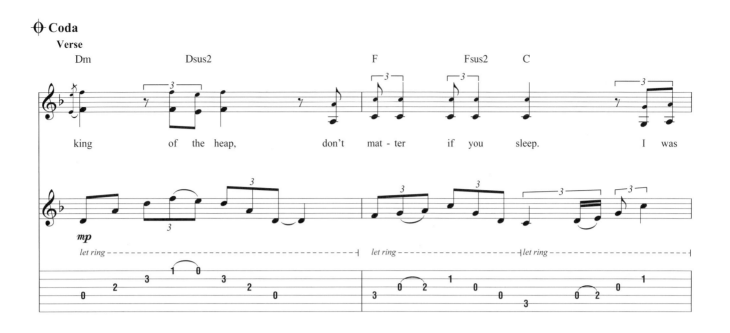

king of the heap, don't mat - ter if you sleep. I was

cool to be steered, thinked and missed, the a-byss is near __ Cham - pagne __ all the read-y; my

hands nev-er stead-y. My head's al - ways down, all a - round I hear the sounds. __ Are you a

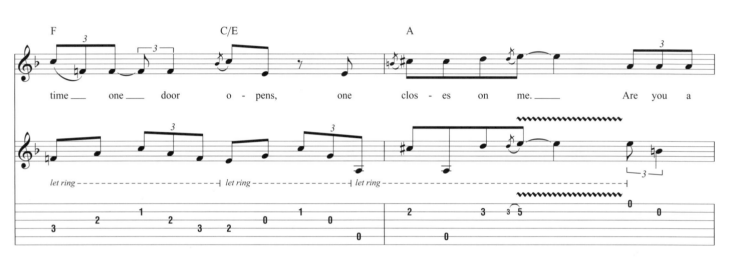

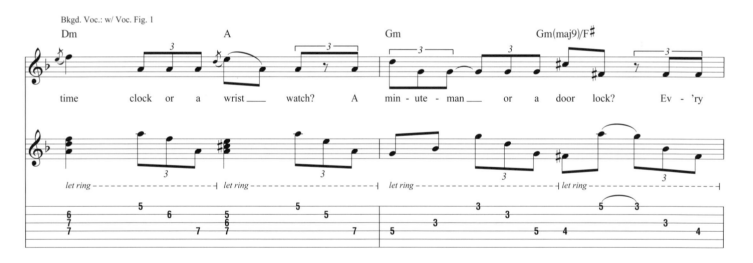

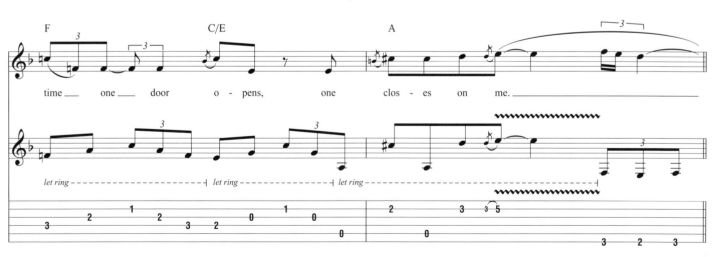

Interlude

Gtr. 1: w/ Riff A

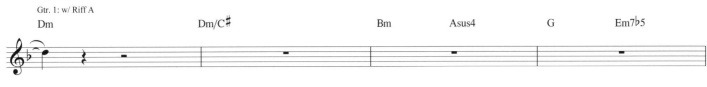

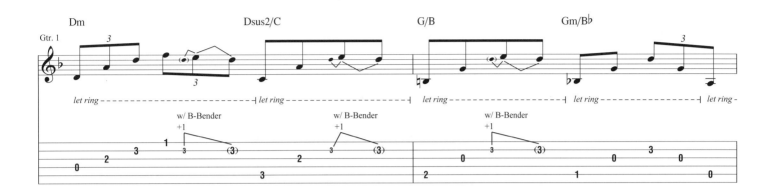

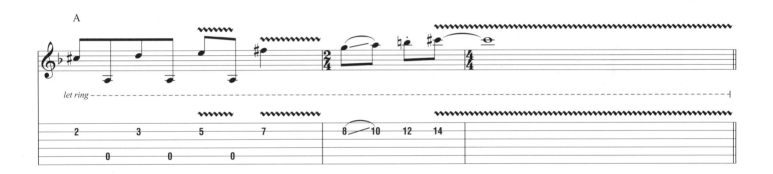

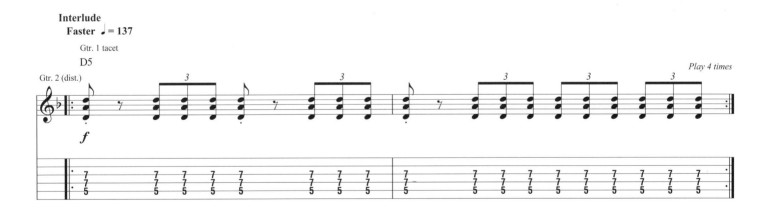

Interlude

Faster ♩ = 137

Gtr. 1 tacet

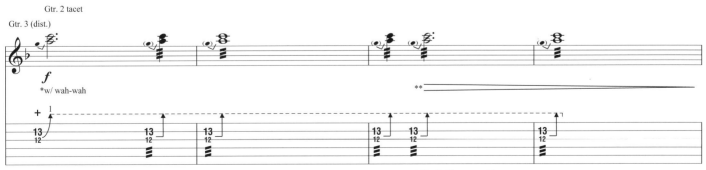

*Wah-wah indications: ⊕ = closed (tow down); ○ = open (toe up)   **Gradually open pedal.

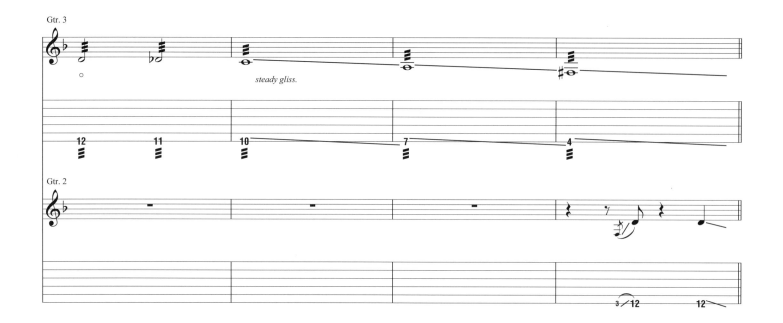

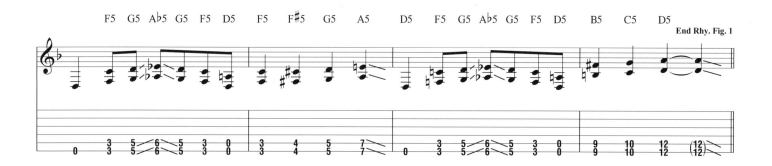

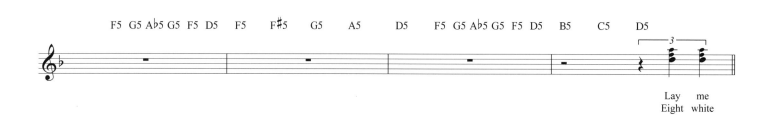

Lay me
Eight white

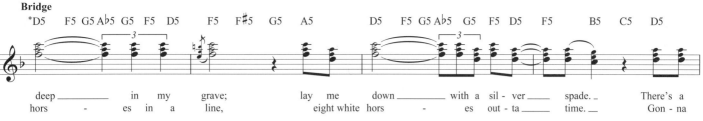

*Chord symbols reflect overall harmony.

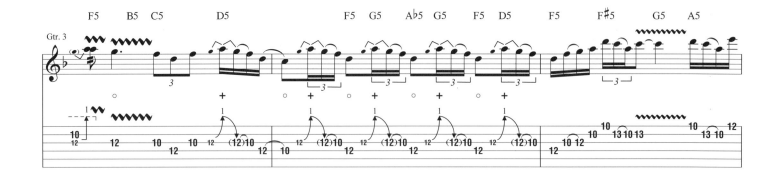

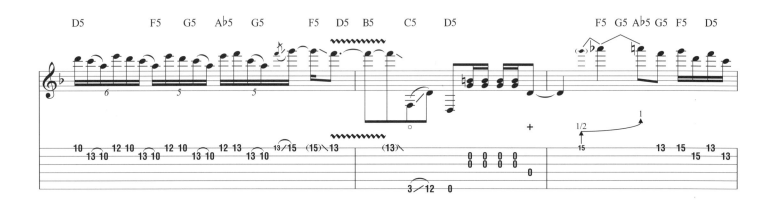

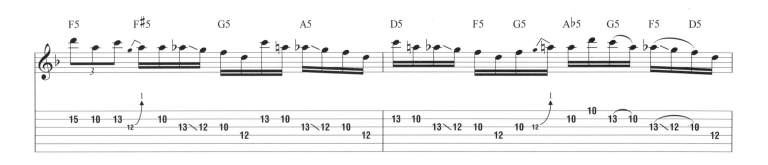

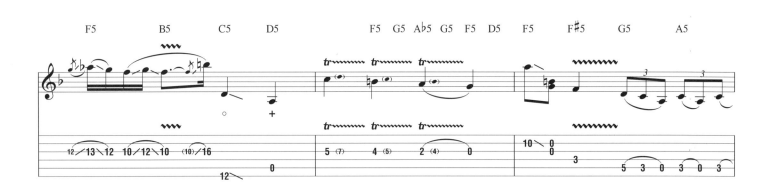

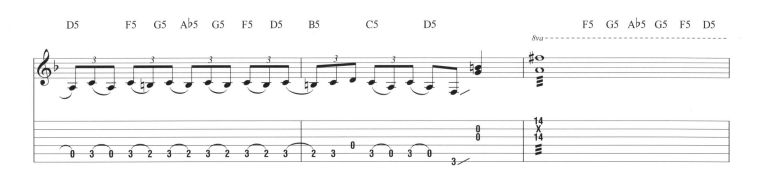

10

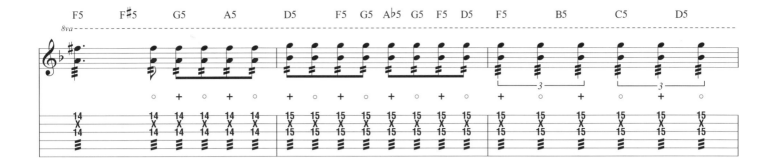

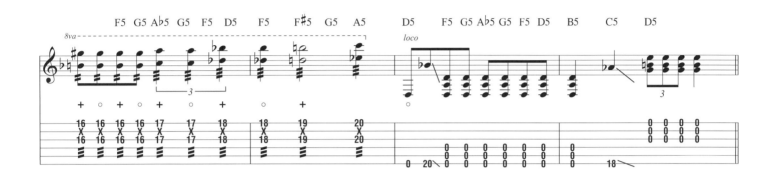

Interlude

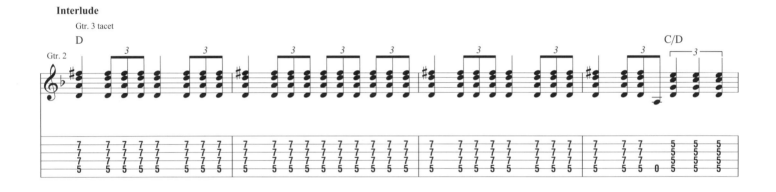

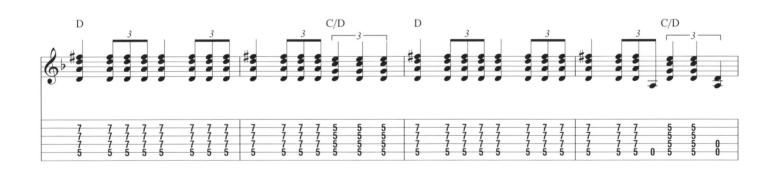

Freely

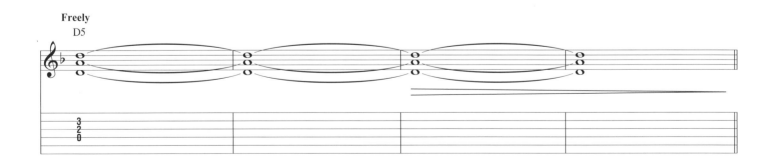

Interlude
Tempo I

Gtr. 2 tacet

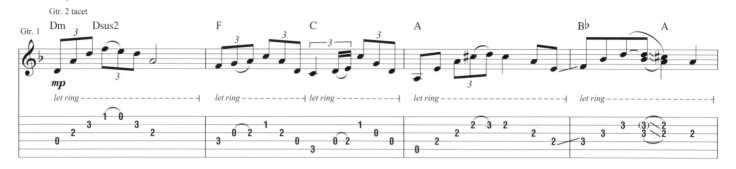

*Played as even eighth-notes.

Outro-Verse

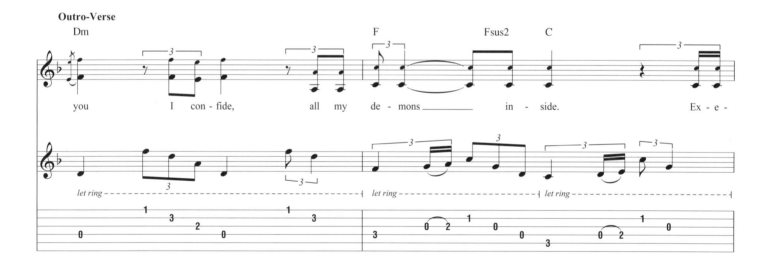

you   I con - fide,   all my de - mons   in - side.   Ex - e -

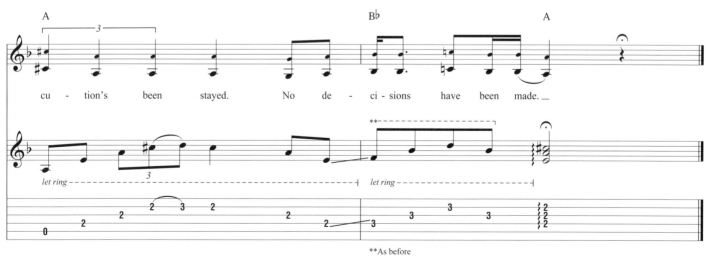

cu - tion's been stayed.   No de - ci - sions have been made.

**As before

Royal Tea

Words and Music by Joe Bonamassa, James House and Kevin Shirley

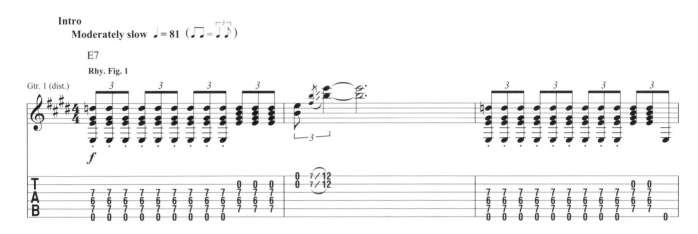

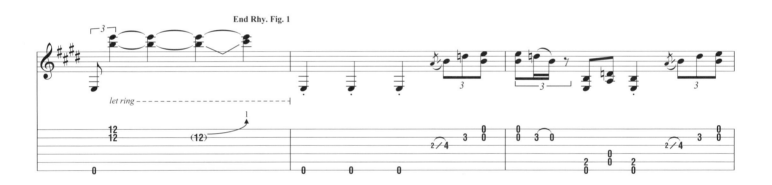

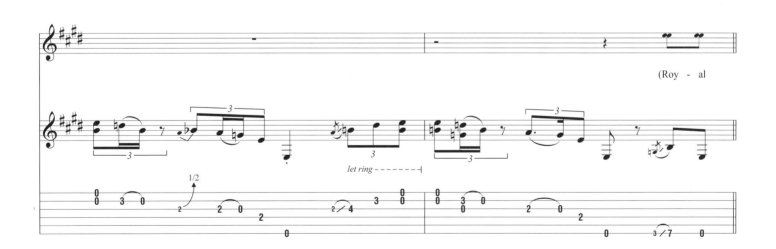

(Roy - al

give you life, all first class, __ let you make your own pho-to-graphs. __

Chan-de-liers and cra-zy cars, paid in full with my __ gui-tars. __

(Roy - al

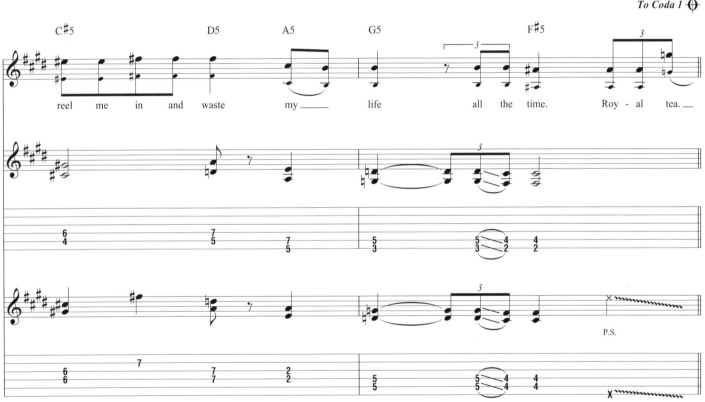

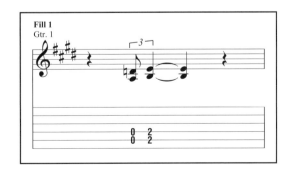

Get - tin' 'way with mur - - der.

tea.)

Gtr. 5 tacet

A7

Break - in' hearts, _ 'round this town, _ mak - in' fools _ of all you clowns. _

Gtr. 1

let ring

P.M.

let ring

P.M.

Ra - zor's edge, my life's a beam ___ the likes of which you've nev - er seen. ___

(Roy - al

⊕ Coda 1

Interlude

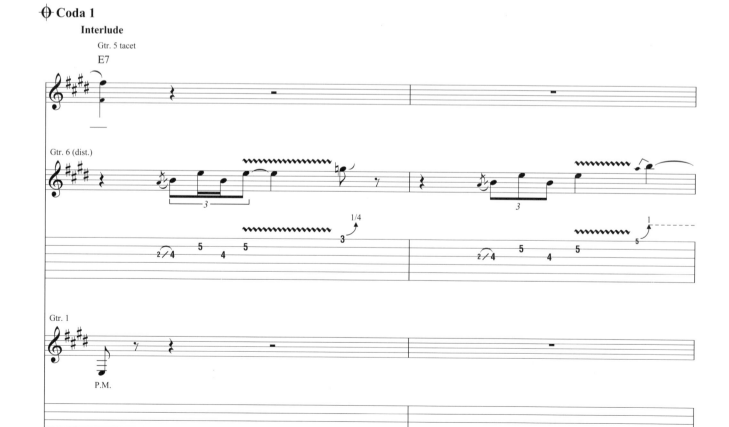

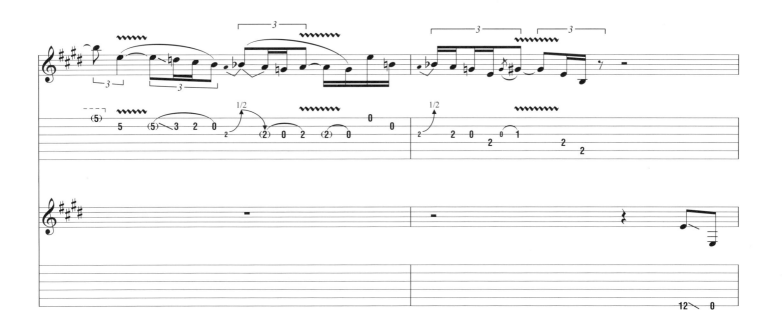

Gtr. 1: w/ Rhy. Fig. 1

Gtr. 6 tacet

Gtr. 7 (dist.)

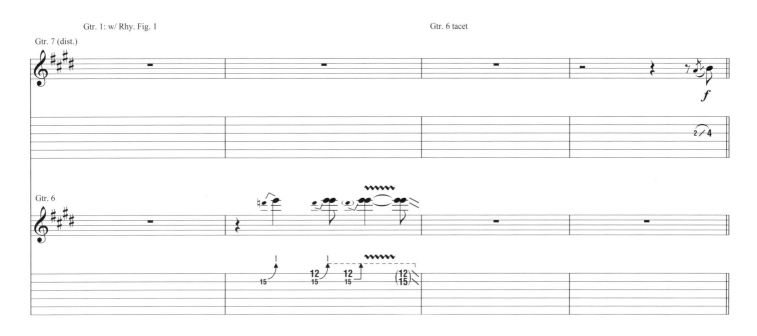

Gtr. 6

Guitar Solo

A7

Gtr. 7

Gtr. 8 (dist.)

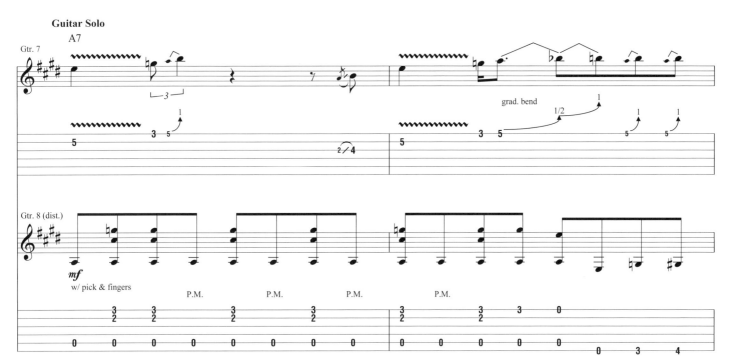

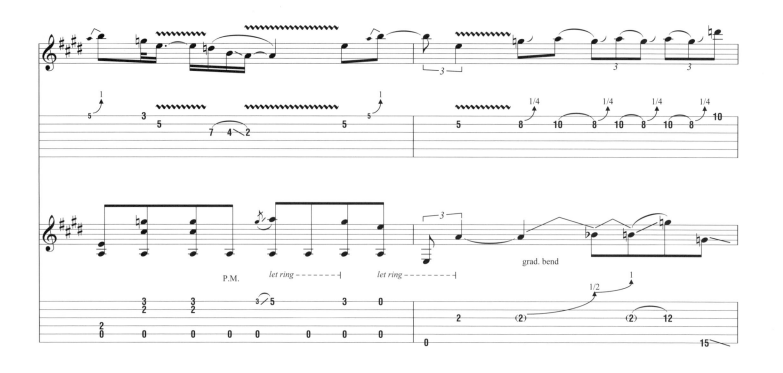

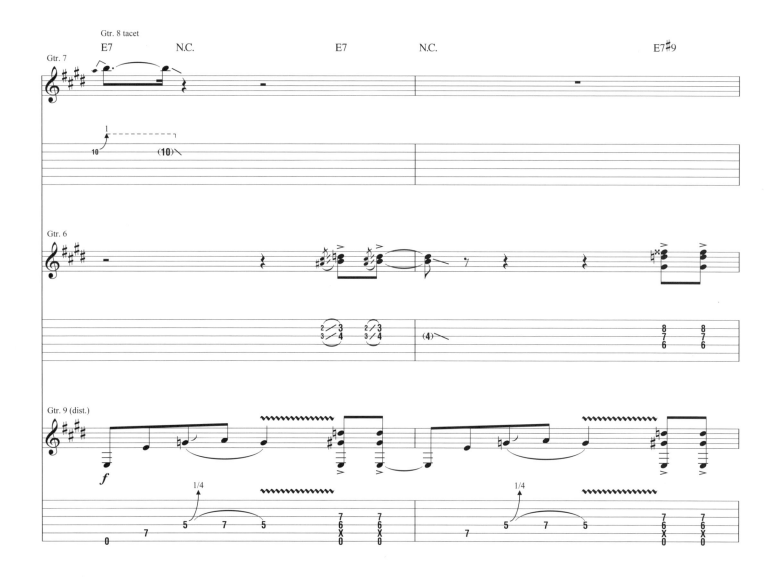

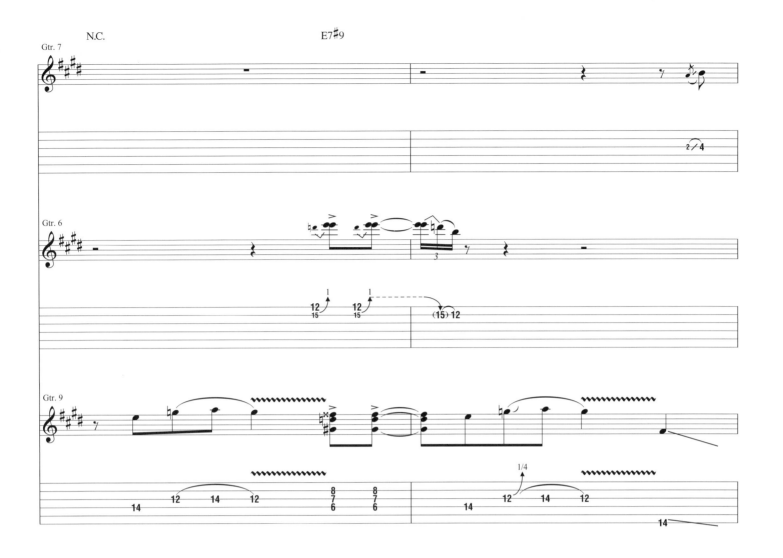

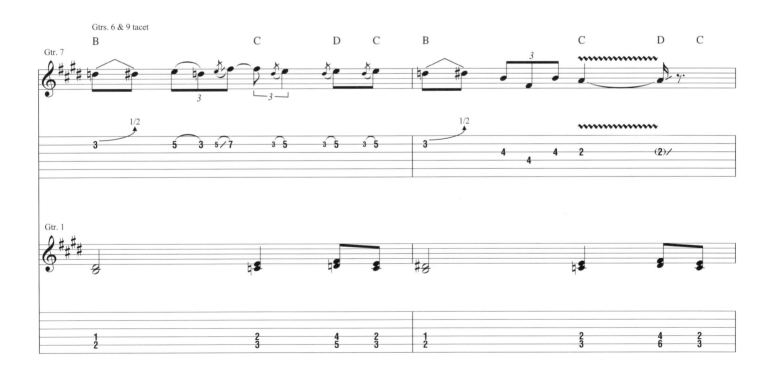

Cham - pagne from the foun - tain.

tea.)

Gtr. 5

Gtr. 1

Verse

Gtr. 5 tacet

A7

3. Hid - in' out   in your pal - ace,   dia - monds drip - pin'   from your chal - ice.

Gtr. 1

P.M.   P.M.

Hon-ey's sweet, but the bees-'ll sting ___ at the door of your reck-on-ing. ___

(Roy - al

⊕ Coda 2

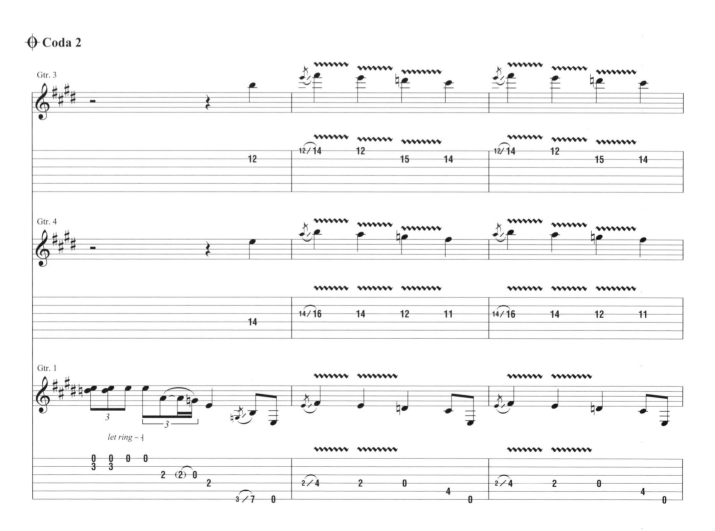

let ring

Why Does It Take So Long to Say Goobye?

Words and Music by Joe Bonamassa and Bernie Marsden

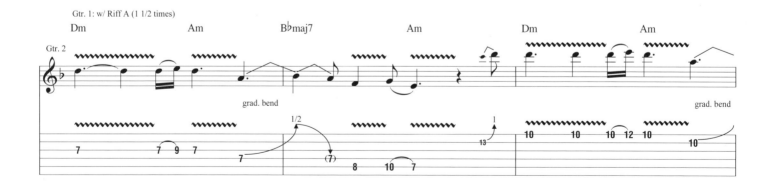

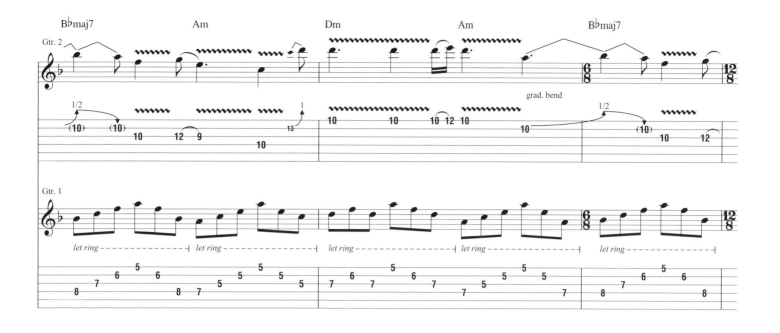

Verse

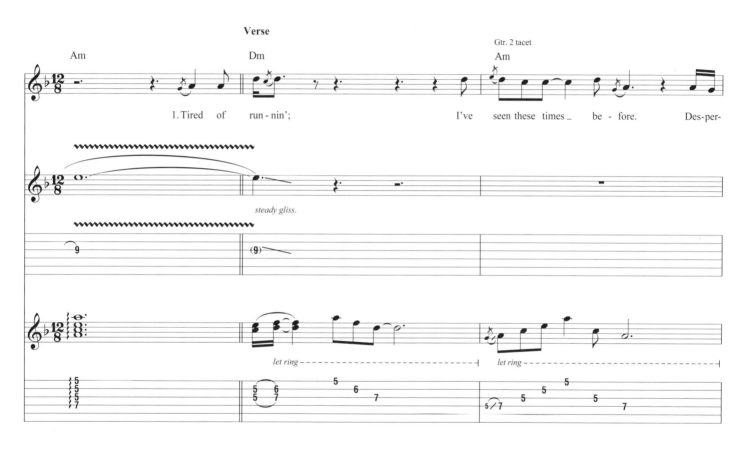

1. Tired of run-nin'; I've seen these times be-fore. Des-per-

a - tion, our can-dle burns no more. Ev-'ry-thing we know takes us

so far _____ a - way. Trace your steps back. _____ Don't let 'em guide your way. When I

*Gtr. 3 (dist.)

*Two gtrs. arr. for one.

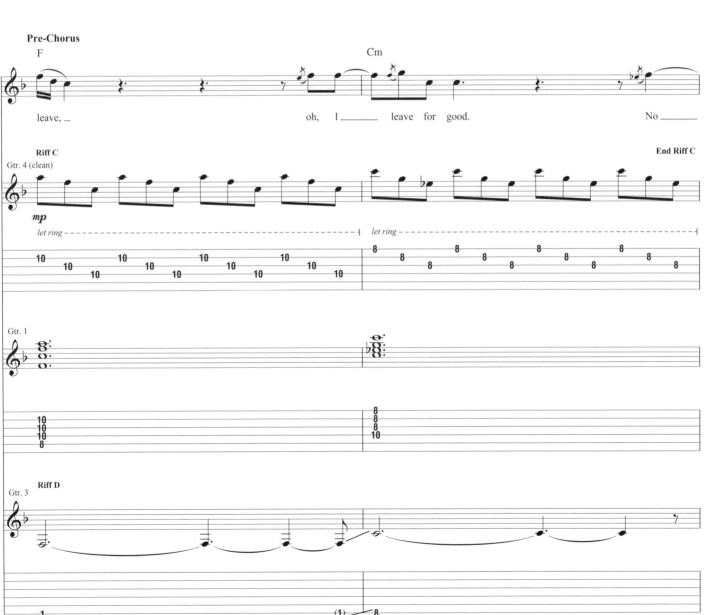

Pre-Chorus

leave, __ oh, I _____ leave for good. _____ No _____

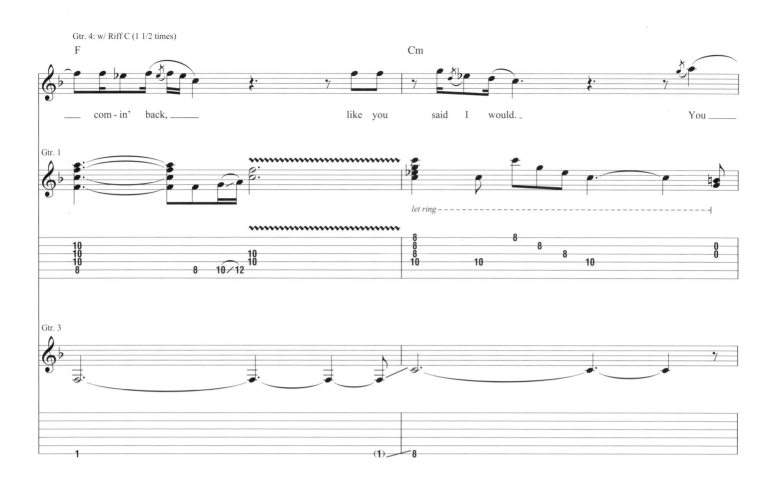

Verse

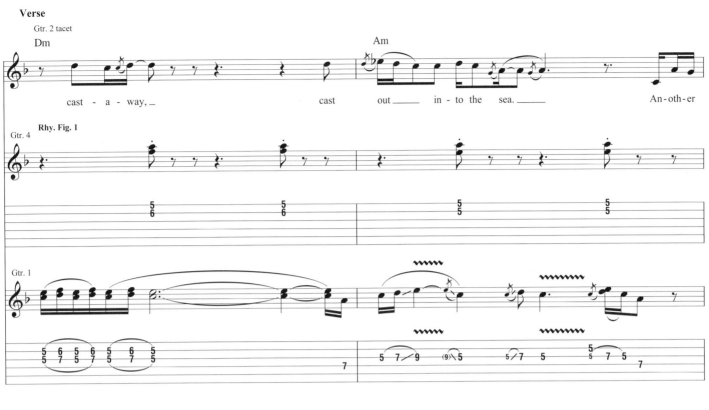

cast - a - way, ___ cast out ___ in - to the sea. ___ An - oth - er

rain - y night, ___ tears from the end - less fights. ___ Oh, I

car - ried you, ___ car - ried you on my own. ___ So

take the love you've had ___ and pre - tend you al - ways know. ___ When I

Pre-Chorus

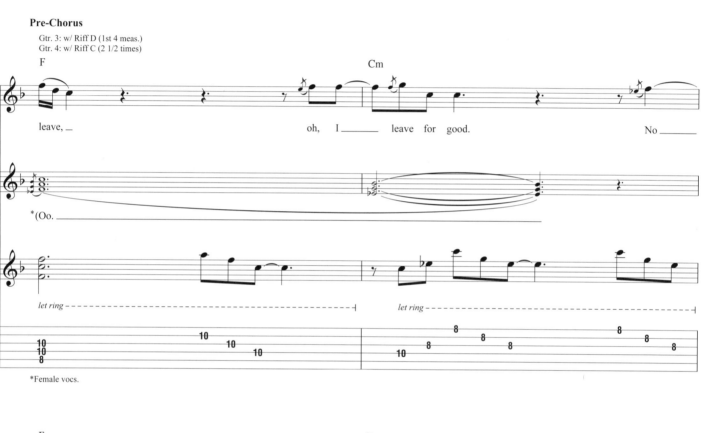

leave, ___ oh, I ___ leave for good. No ___

*(Oo. ___

*Female vocs.

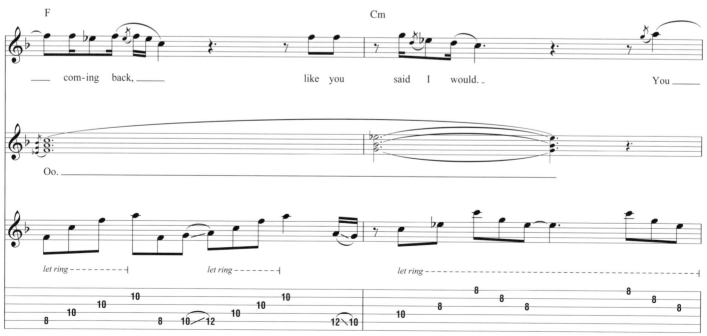

___ com-ing back, ___ like you said I would. ___ You ___

Oo.

Interlude

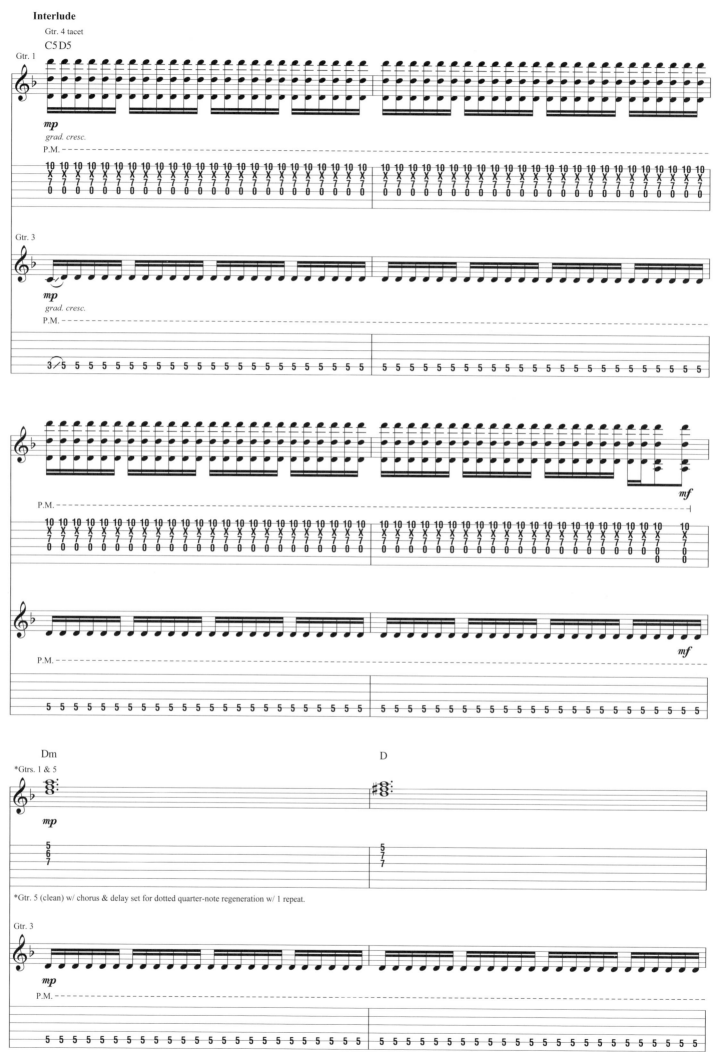

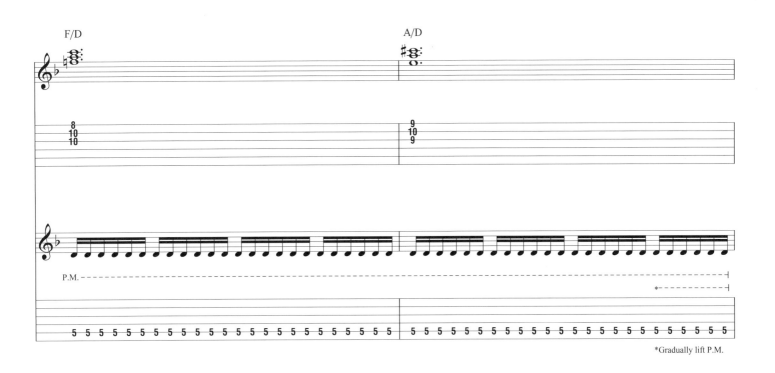

*Gradually lift P.M.

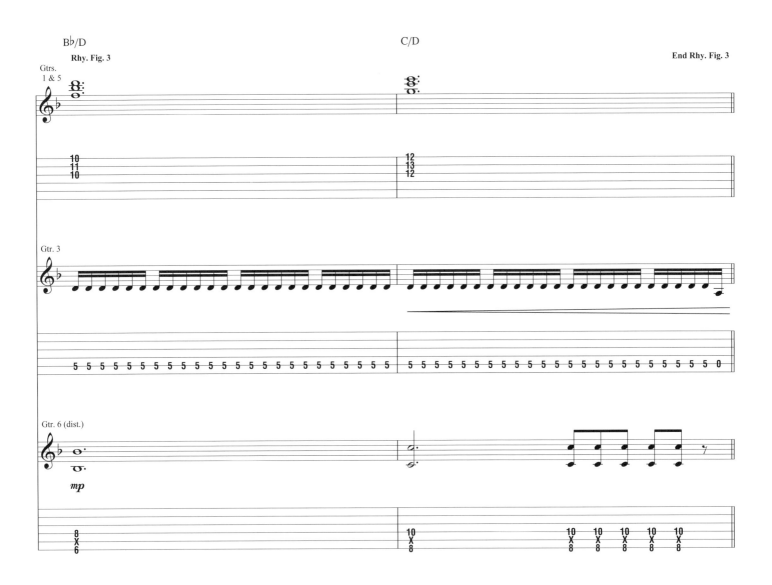

Interlude

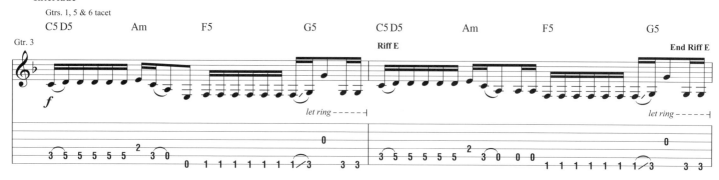

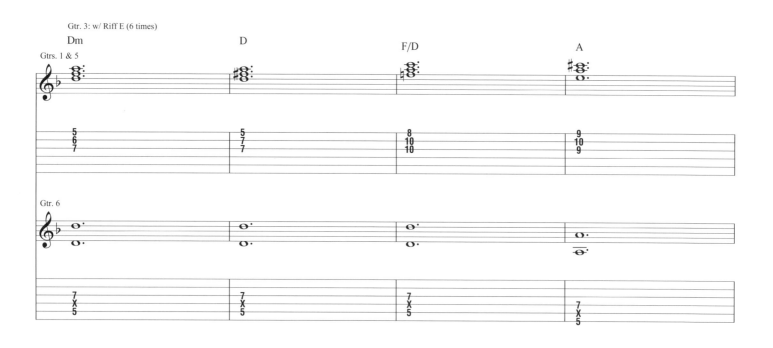

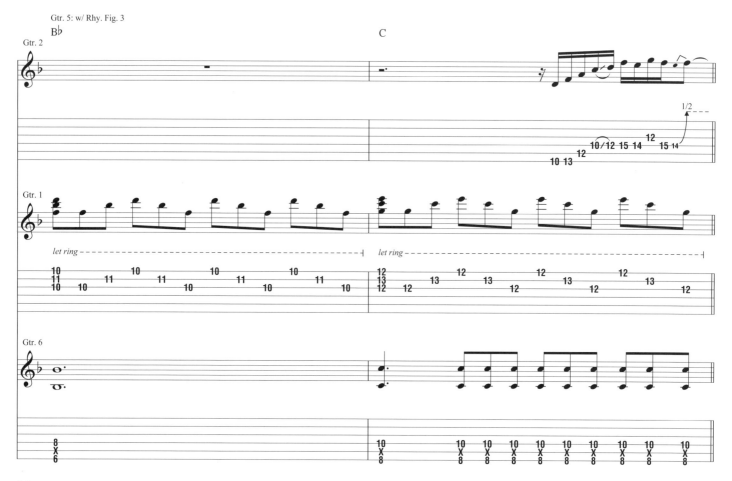

Guitar Solo

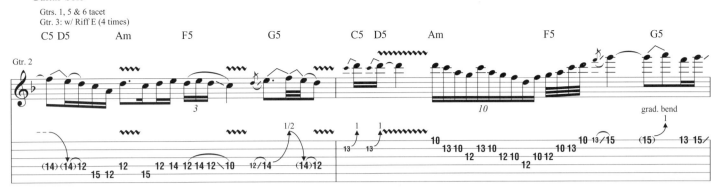

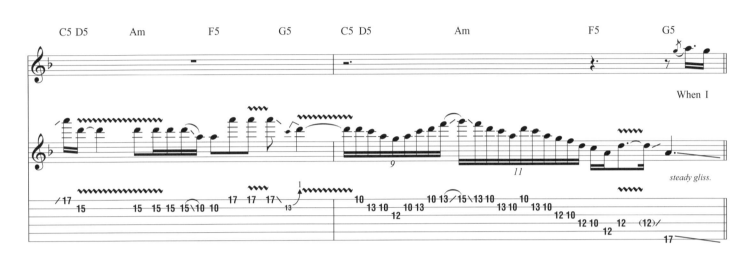

Pre-Chorus

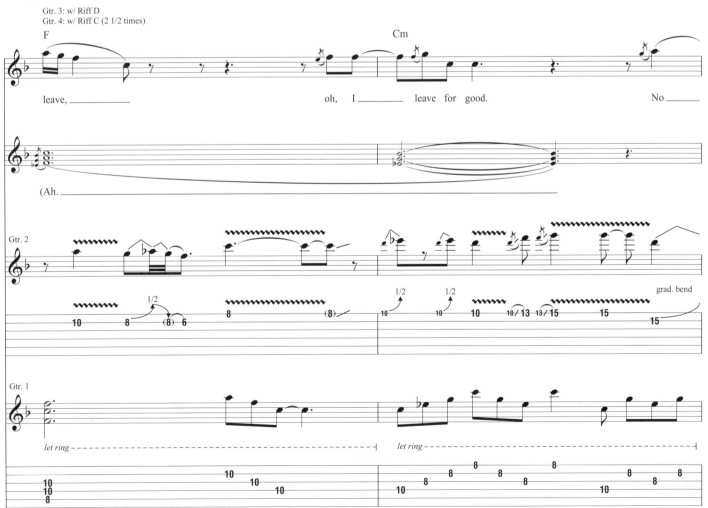

Interlude

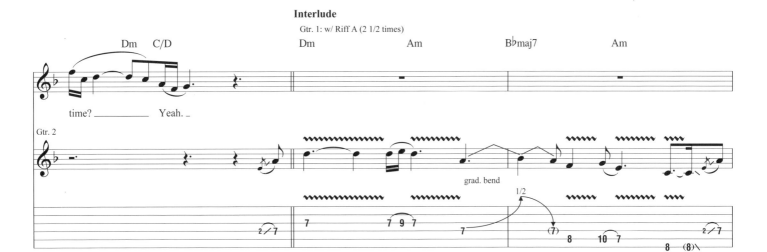

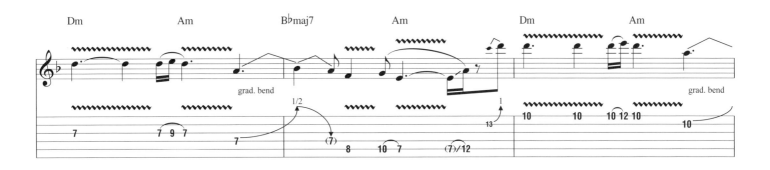

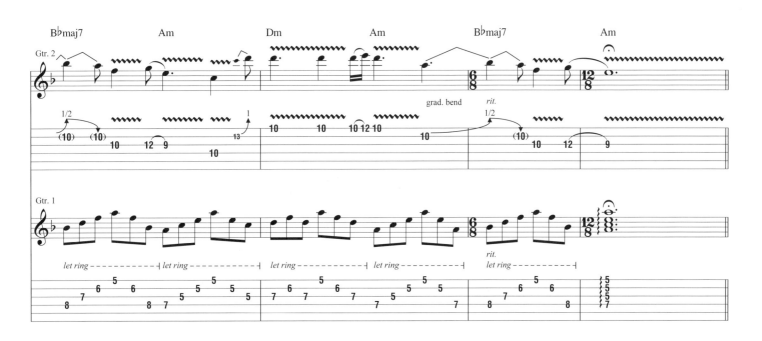

Lookout Man

Words and Music by Joe Bonamassa, Peter Brown, Kevin Shirley and Mike McCully

Tune down 1 1/2 steps:
(low to high) C#-F#-B-E-G#-C#

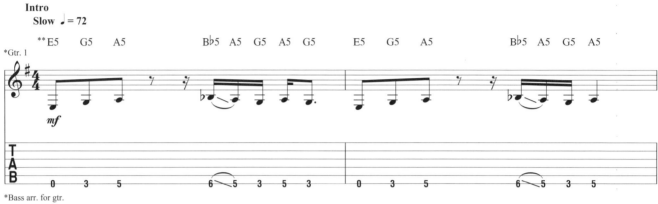

*Bass arr. for gtr.

**Chord symbols reflect implied harmony.

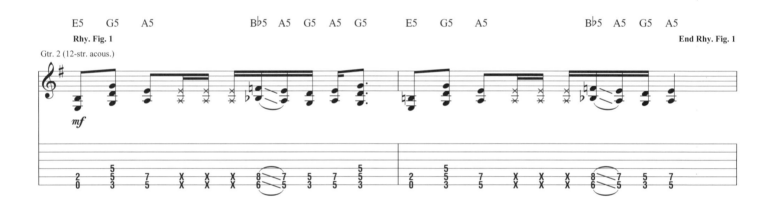

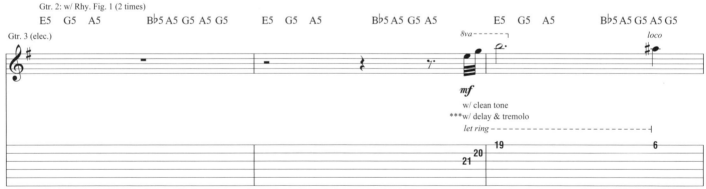

***Delay set for quarter-note regeneration w/ 1 repeat.

Gtrs. 4 & 5: w/ Riff A (2 times)

1st time, Gtr. 3 tacet

E5   G5   A5   Bb5 A5 G5 A5 G5   E5   G5   A5   Bb5 A5 G5 A5

let ring

Bkgd. Voc.: w/ Voc. Fig. 1

E5   G5   A5   Bb5 A5 G5 A5 G5   E5   G5   A5   Bb5 A5 G5 A5

𝄌 Verse

Gtr. 3: w/ Rhy. Fig. 1 (2 times)
Gtr. 6: w/ Riff B (2 times)

E5   G5   A5   Bb5 A5 G5 A5 G5   E5   G5   A5   Bb5 A5 G5 A5

2. Look out,   man,   I'm   com-ing from big scene.   Look out,   man,   steak   frite and bur - gun - dy.
4. Look out,   man,   I'm as quick as   I am fast.   Look out,   man,   just   ask   the Cave-man.
5. Look out,   man,   I'm the one who can't be beat.   Look out,   man,   I'm the one who won't re - peat.

2nd time, Gtr. 4: w/ Fill 2
2nd time, Gtr. 5: w/ Fill 3

E5   G5   A5   Bb5 A5 G5 A5 G5   E5   G5   A5   Bb5 A5 G5 A5

Look out,   peo-ple, I'm   com-ing from the sun.   Look out,   peo-ple, it's   good for ev - 'ry - one.
Look out,   peo-ple, don't   keep me in   a cage.   Look out,   peo-ple, the   storm a - bout to rage.
Look out,   peo-ple, I'm   lean,   mean and dazed.   Look out,   peo-ple, I'm the one who won't be fazed.

Gtr. 4   Fill 1   End Fill 1

Gtrs. 4 & 5: w/ Riff A

E5   G5   A5   Bb5 A5 G5 A5 G5   E5   G5   A5   Bb5 A5 G5 A5

Fill 2
Gtr. 4

mp

P.S.

Fill 3
Gtr. 5

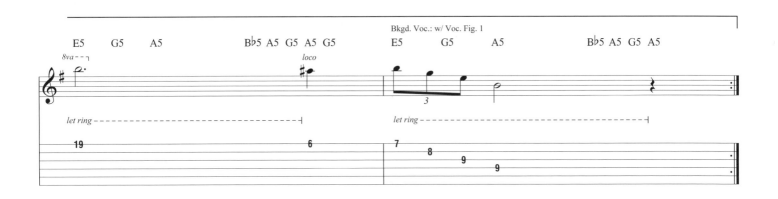

*w/ echo (as before)

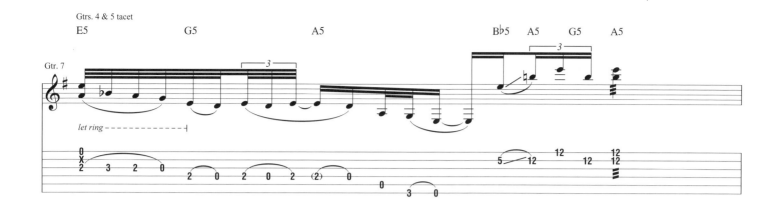

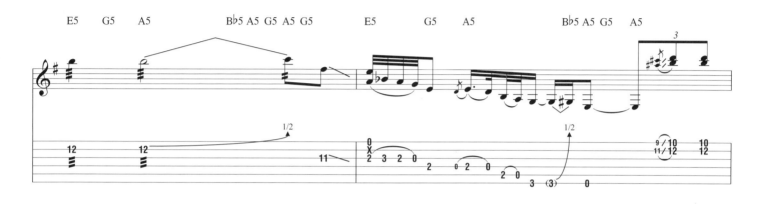

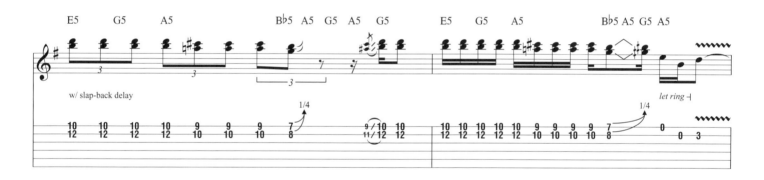

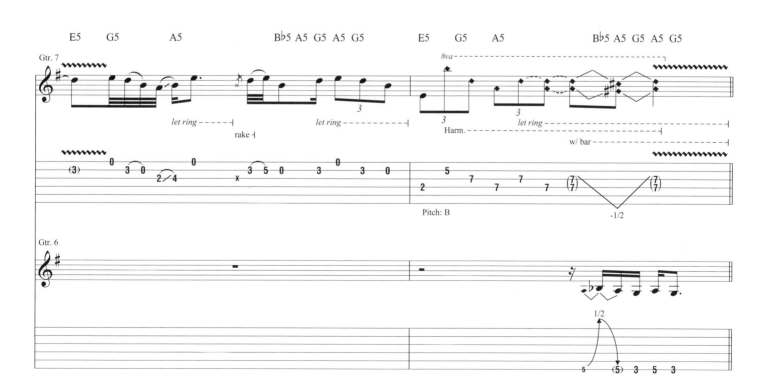

Harmonica Solo

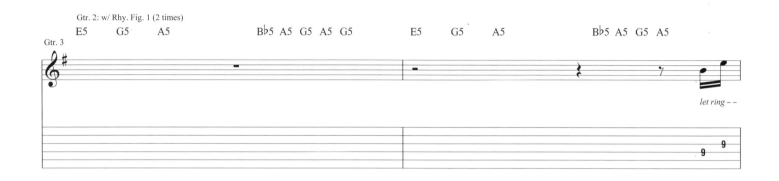

D.S. al Coda

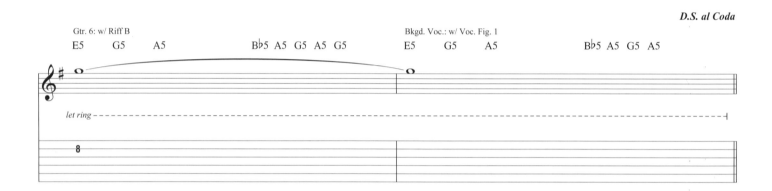

*Composite arrangement

High Class Girl

Words and Music by Joe Bonamassa and Bernie Marsden

Intro
Moderately ♩ = 120

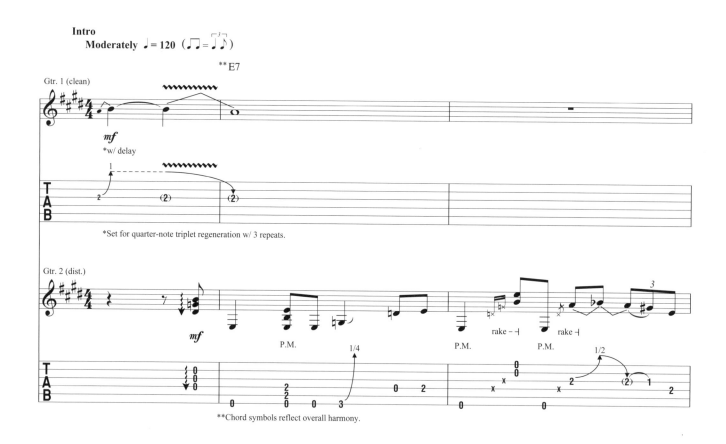

*Set for quarter-note triplet regeneration w/ 3 repeats.

**Chord symbols reflect overall harmony.

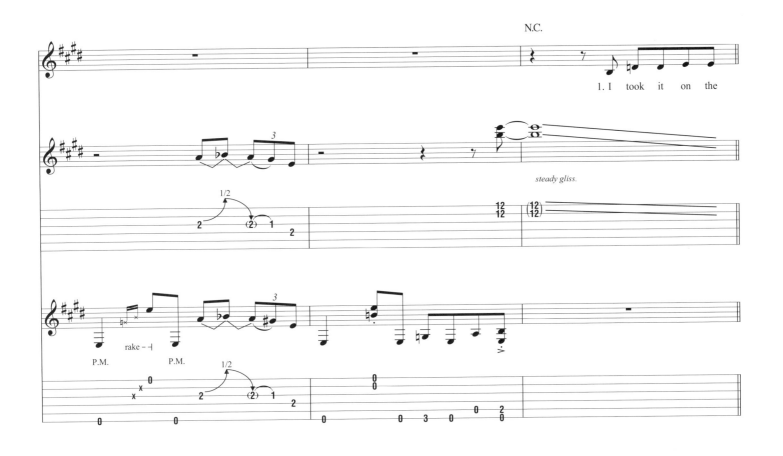

Verse

Gtr. 1 tacet

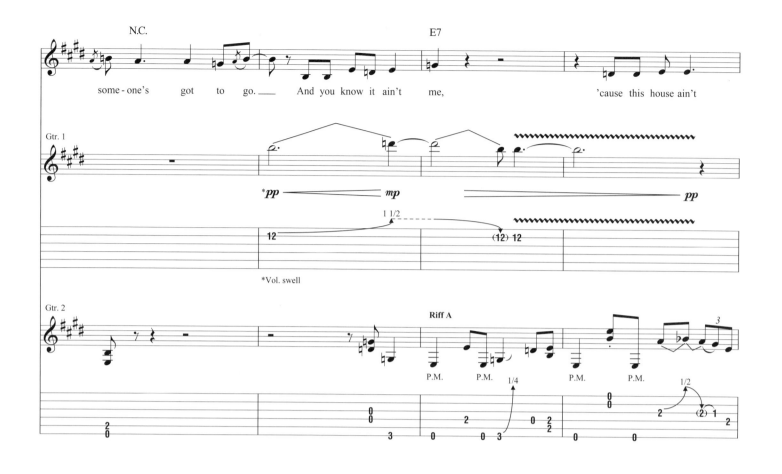

some - one's got to go.____ And you know it ain't me, 'cause this house ain't

free.____ When you choose to ____ lie ____ and you

take his side. That's the way it's gon - na be.____ 'Cause I'm no - bod - y's

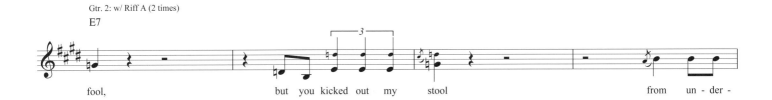

Gtr. 2: w/ Riff A (2 times)

fool, but you kicked out my stool from un-der-

N.C.

neath my life. Ya made a mess this time, but do what you got to do.

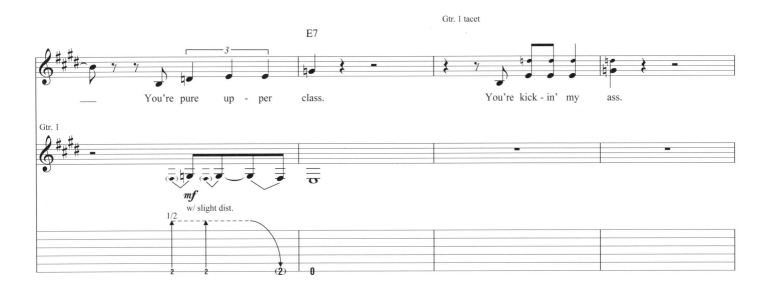

Gtr. 1 tacet

E7

You're pure up - per class. You're kick-in' my ass.

Gtr. 1

mf
w/ slight dist.

N.C.

You took your time twist-in' the knife once in-side my heart that's beat-in' fast,

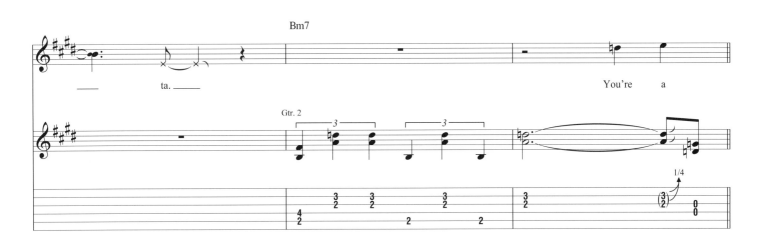

Bm7

ta. You're a

Gtr. 2

Chorus

Gtr. 2: w/ Riff A

E7

high - class girl, low - class ways. If I

stay an - y long - er and I sit and I pon - der, gon - na throw it all a - way. ___

Interlude

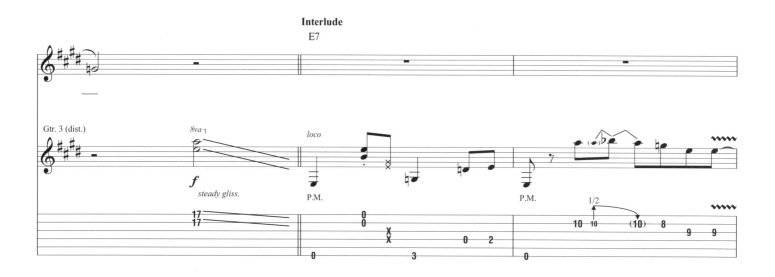

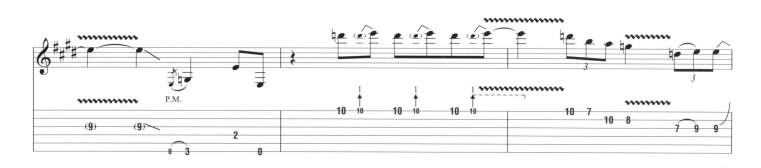

2. I'd be in the

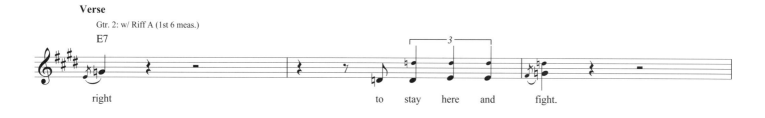

right   to   stay   here   and   fight.

So break it down for me ___ like a child, you see. For the

wrong rea - sons, you are right. ___ Bring on the mo -

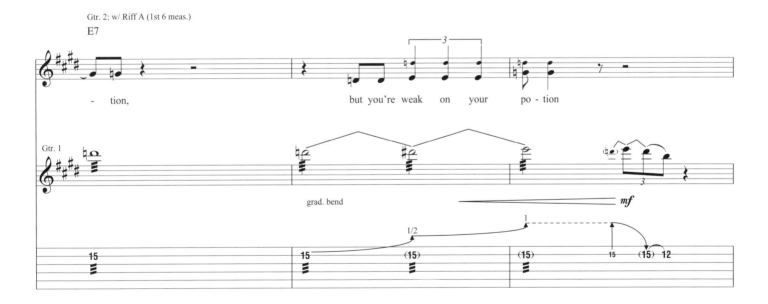

- tion, but you're weak on your po - tion

to keep me a - round af - ter you beat me down. Ba - by, I

rev - el in ___ your de - vo - tion.

You're a

Chorus

Gtr. 2: w/ Riff A (1st 6 meas.)

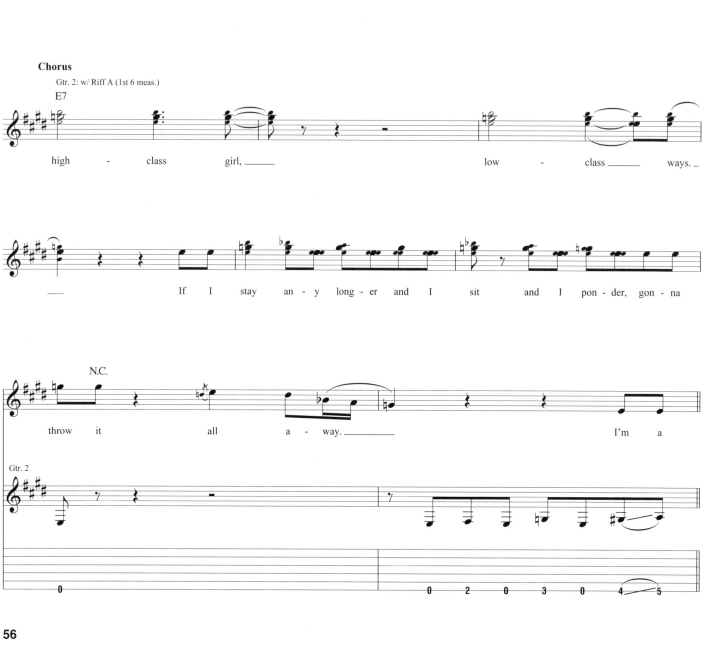

high - class girl, ___ low - class ___ ways. ___

If I stay an - y long - er and I sit and I pon - der, gon - na

throw it all a - way. ___

I'm a

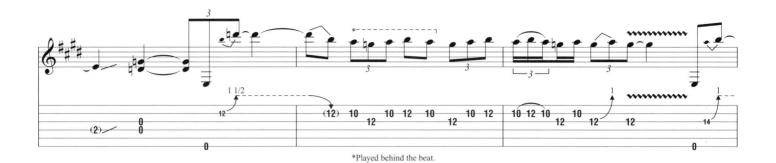

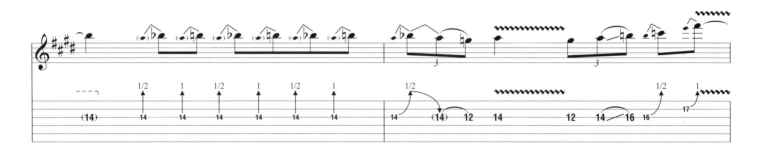

*Played behind the beat.

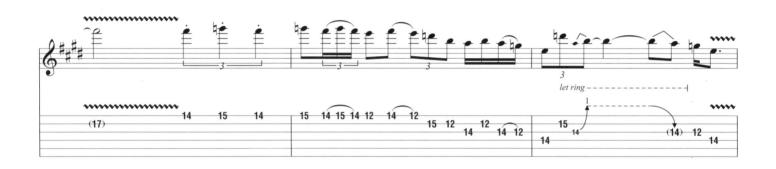

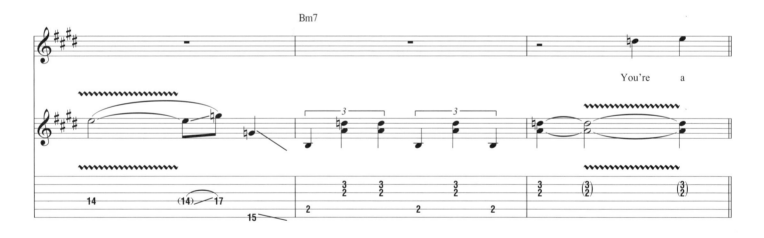

Bm7

You're a

Chorus

Gtr. 2: w/ Riff A (1st 4 meas., 3 times)
Gtr. 3 tacet

E7

high - class girl, _____ low - class _____ ways. _____ If I

stay an - y long - er and sit and I pon - der, gon - na throw it all a - way. _____ You're a

high - class girl, ___ low - class ___ ways. ___ If I

stay an - y long-er and sit and I pon-der, gon - na throw it all a - way. ___

Gtr. 4 (dist.)

mf

Gtr. 2

P.M.

P.M. P.M.

let ring - - - - - - -

Outro

E7

Throw it all a - way. ___

(High - class girl. ___

Gtr. 4 **Riff B**

End Riff B

Gtr. 2

P.M. - - - - - - - - - - - - -

let ring - - -

P.M.

A Conversation with Alice

Words and Music by Joe Bonamassa and Bernie Marsden

Gtrs. 4, 7 & 9: Open A tuning:
(low to high) E-A-E-A-C#-E

Intro
Moderately ♩ = 138

*Gtrs. 1, 2 & 3 (dist.)

*Composite arrangement

**Chord symbols reflect basic harmony.

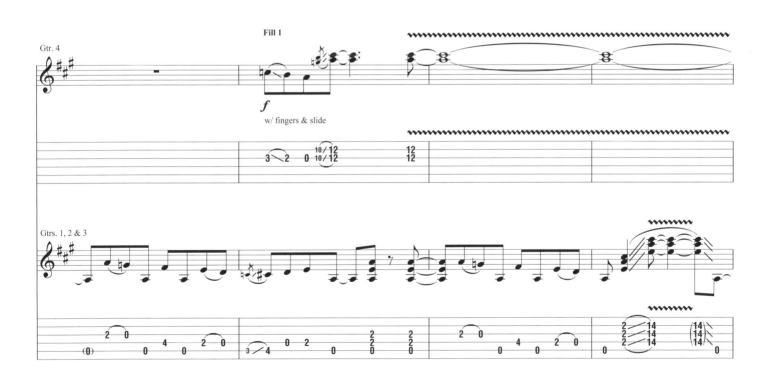

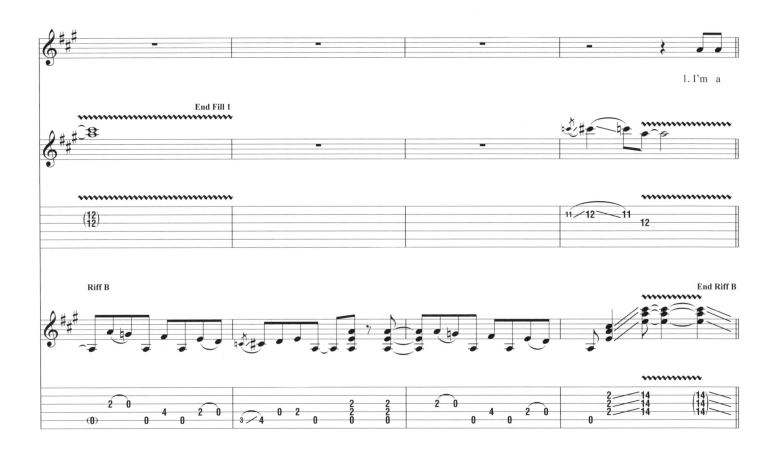

Verse
Half-time feel

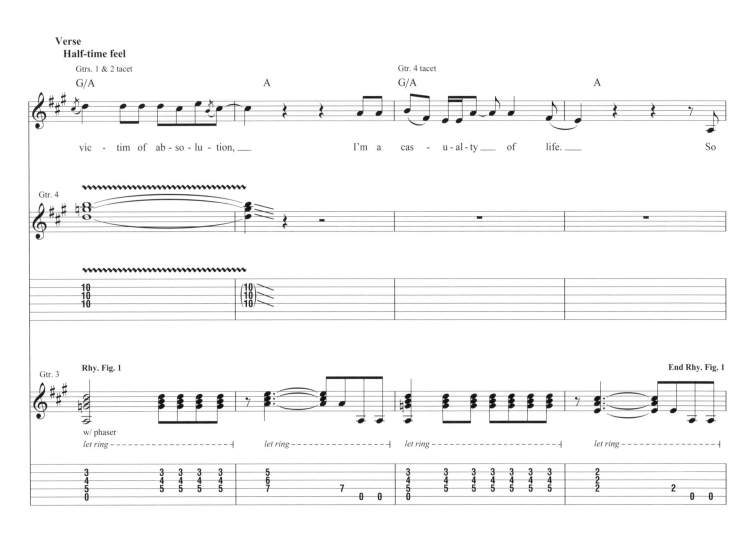

vic - tim of ab - so - lu - tion, ___ I'm a cas - u - al - ty ___ of life. ___ So

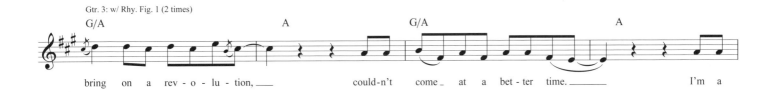

bring on a rev - o - lu - tion, _____ could-n't come _ at a bet - ter time. _____ I'm a

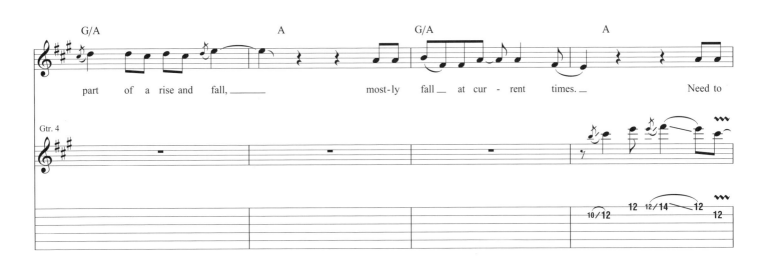

part of a rise and fall, _____ most-ly fall _ at cur - rent times. _ Need to

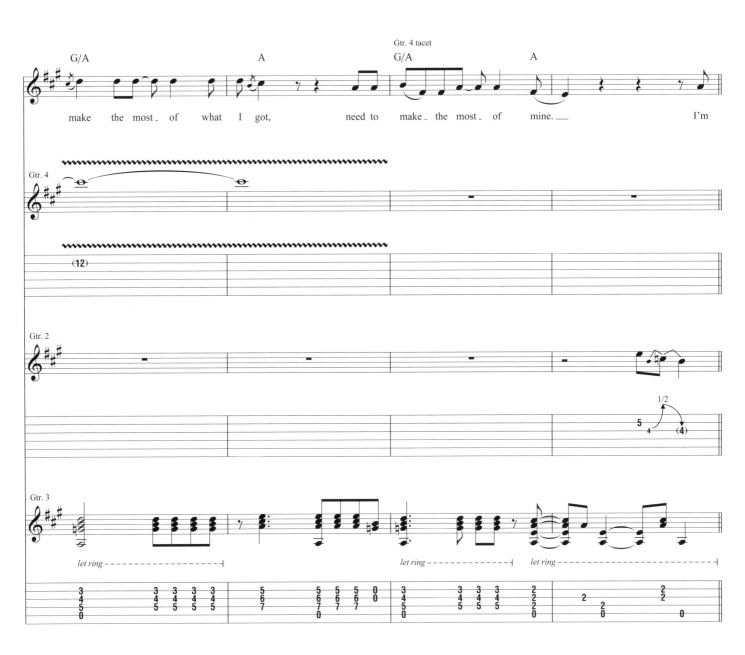

make the most _ of what I got, need to make _ the most _ of mine. _ I'm

*Composite arrangement; Gtr. 5 played *p*.

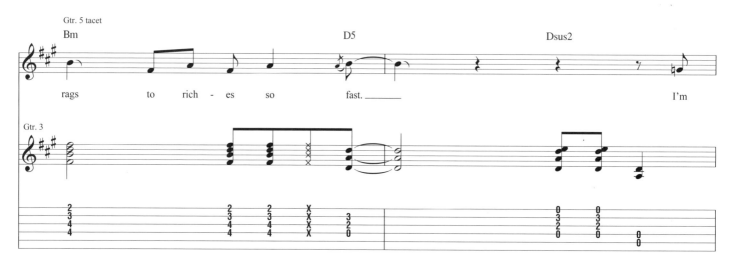

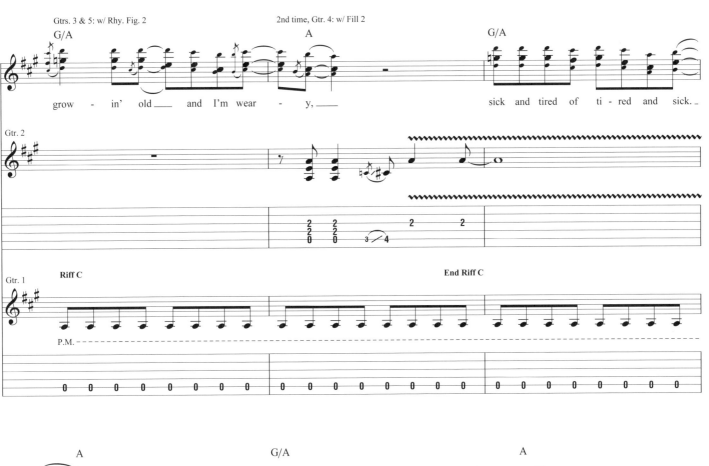

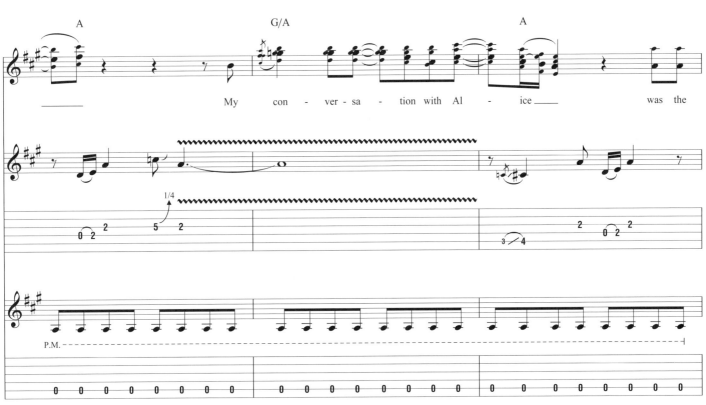

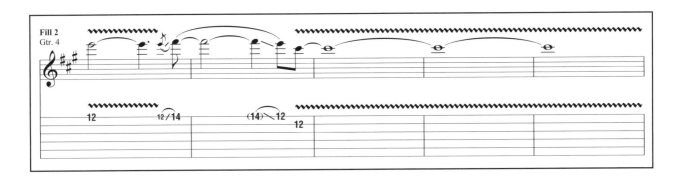

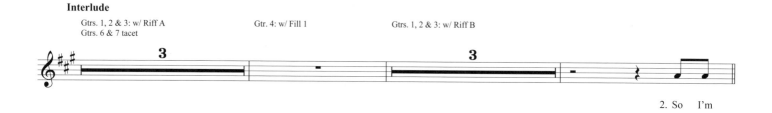

Verse

Gtr. 3: w/ Rhy. Fig. 1 (2 times)

stick-ing to my ___ ex - cus - es, ___ found - in' out who's ___ to blame. ___

All I see is the man in the mir - ror; all I

Gtr. 4

w/o slide

let ring -

D.S. al Coda

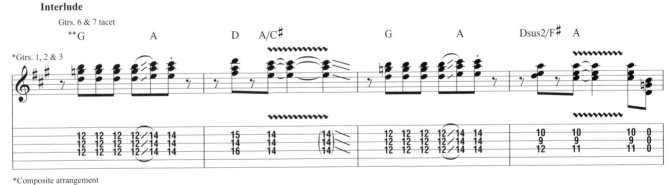

Gtr. 4 tacet

see is more ___ the same. ___ I'm

Gtr. 2

Coda

Interlude

Gtrs. 6 & 7 tacet

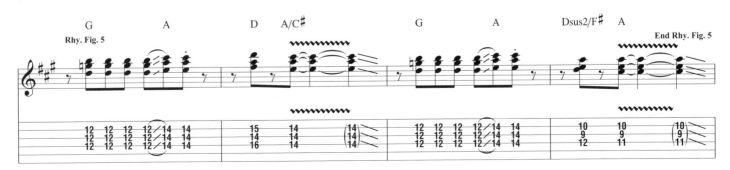

*Gtrs. 1, 2 & 3

*Composite arrangement

**Chord symbols reflect overall harmony.

Rhy. Fig. 5

End Rhy. Fig. 5

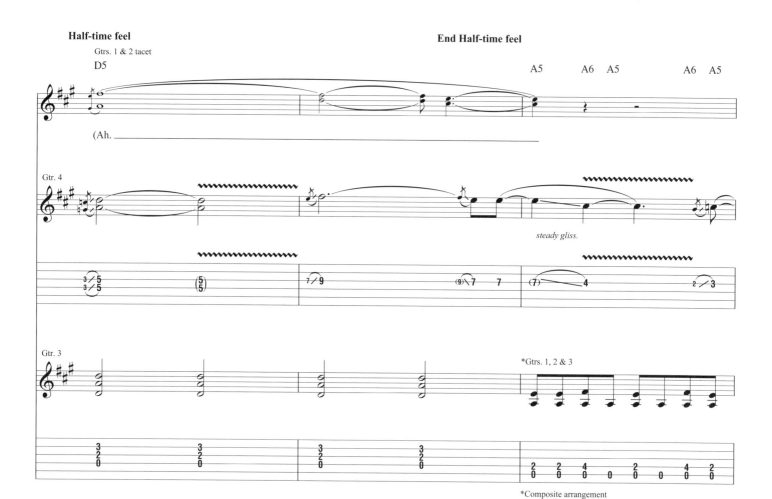

*Composite arrangement

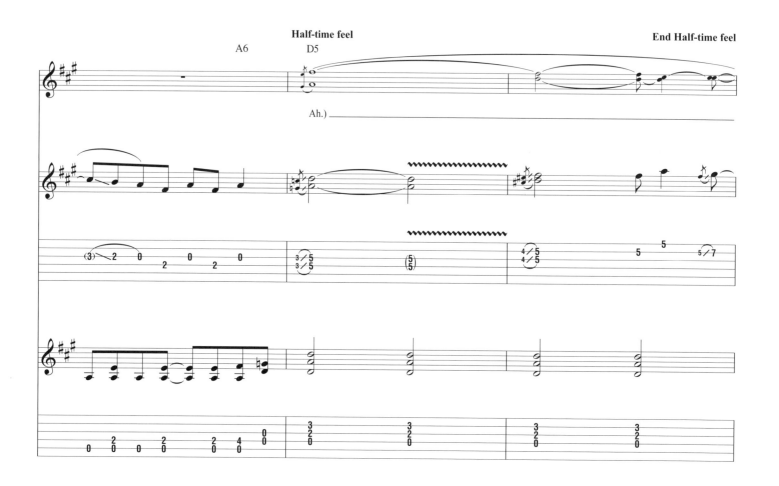

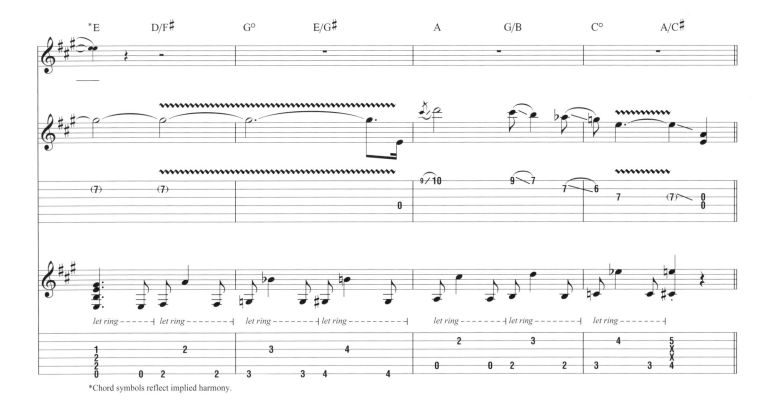

*Chord symbols reflect implied harmony.

Guitar Solo

Gtrs. 1, 2 & 3: w/ Rhy. Fig. 5 (4 times)
Gtr. 4 tacet

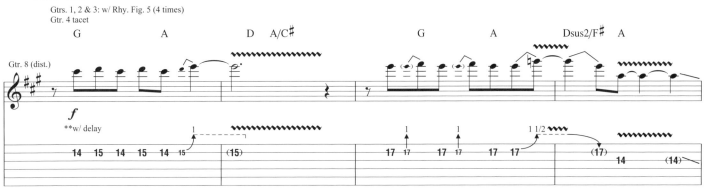

**Set for quarter-note regeneration w/ 2 repeats.

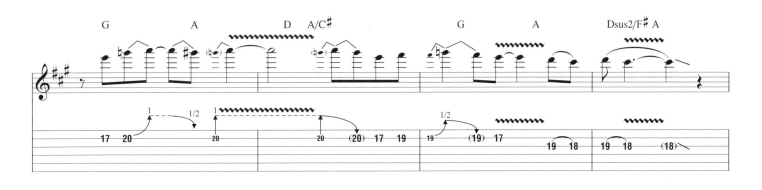

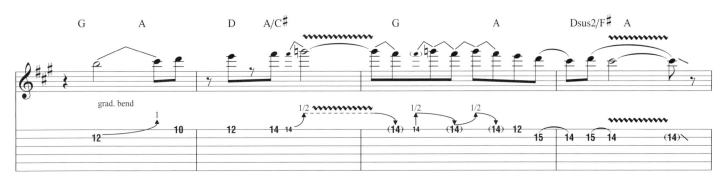

con - ver - sa - tion with Al - ice, my con - ver - sa - tion with Al -

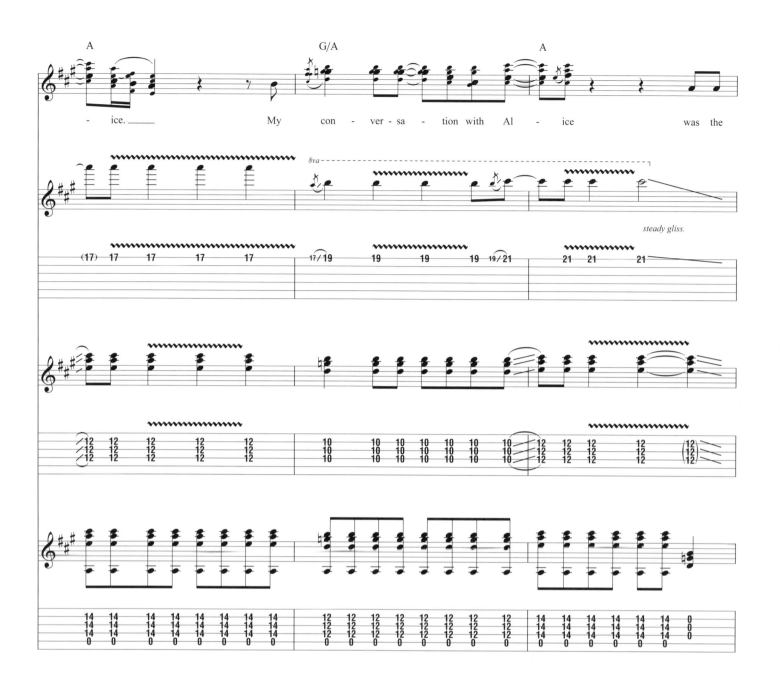

*Composite arrangement

Outro

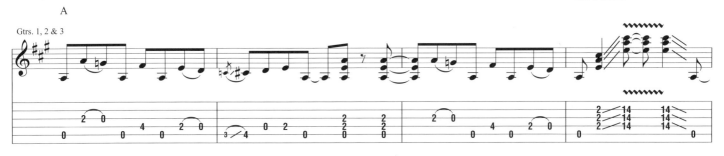

Free time

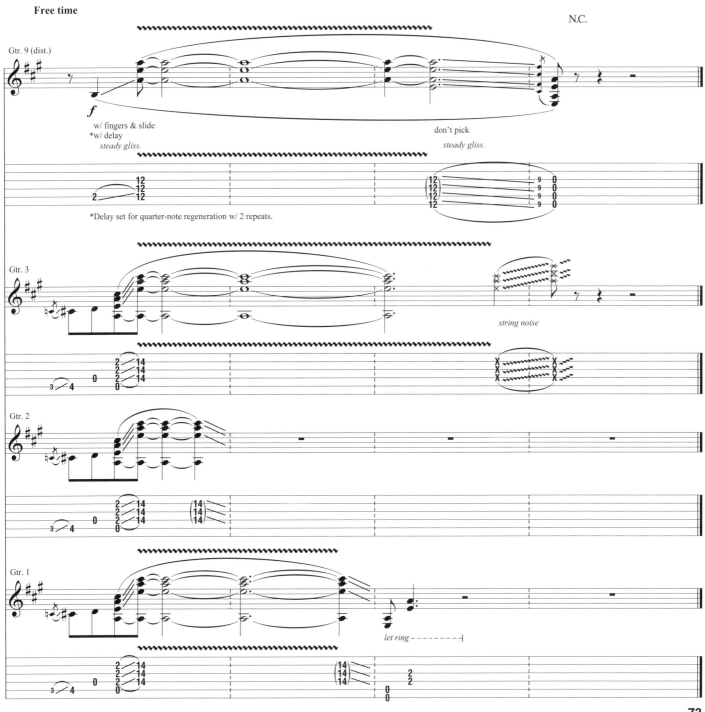

I Didn't Think She Would Do It

Words and Music by Joe Bonamassa, Peter Brown and Bernie Marsden

Intro
Moderately fast ♩ = 145

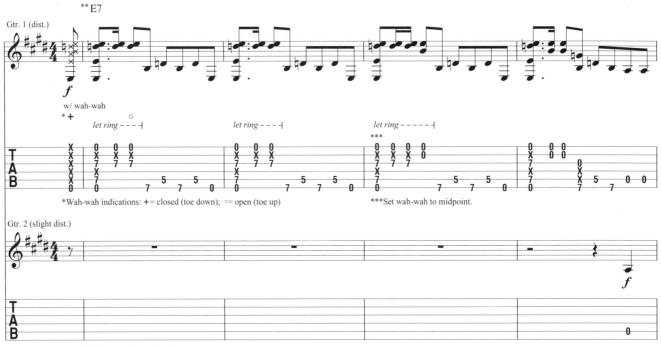

*Wah-wah indications: += closed (toe down); ○= open (toe up)   ***Set wah-wah to midpoint.

**Chord symbols reflect basic harmony.

†Set for quarter-note regeneration w/ 1 repeat.

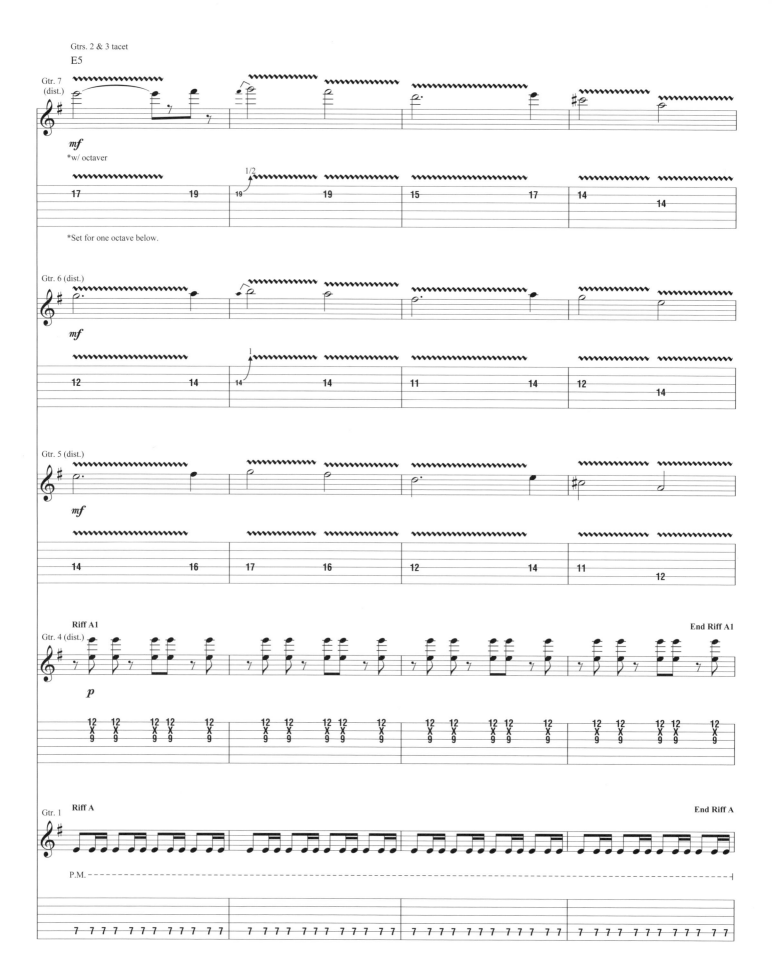

Verse

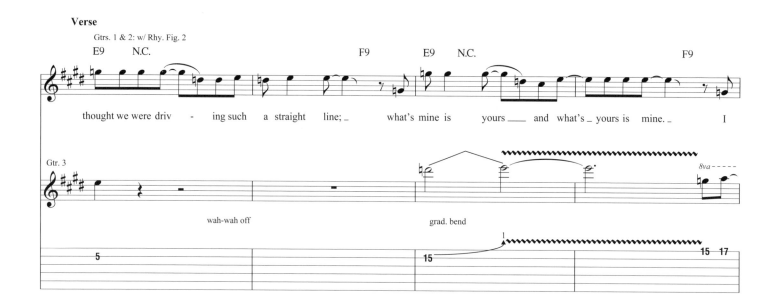

thought we were driv - ing such a straight line;___ what's mine is yours ___ and what's ___ yours is mine.___ I

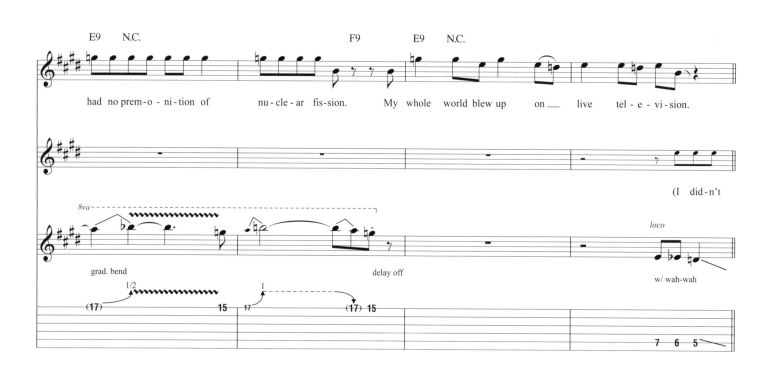

had no prem-o - ni-tion of nu - cle-ar fis-sion. My whole world blew up on ___ live tel-e - vi-sion.

(I did-n't

Chorus

think she would do ___ it. I did-n't think she would do ___ it. _____ I did-n't

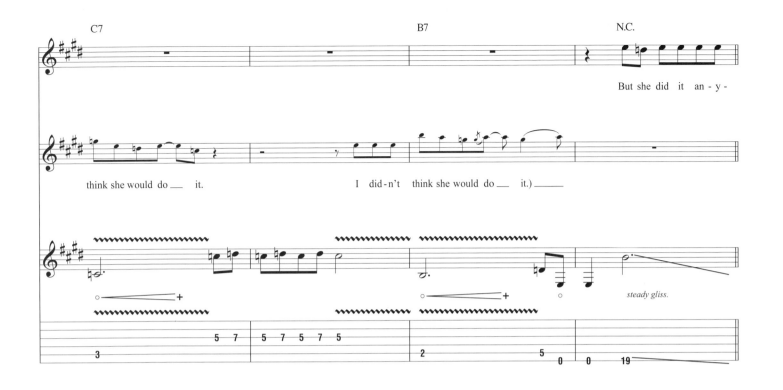

But she did it an-y-

think she would do __ it. I did-n't think she would do __ it.) _____

steady gliss.

Gtr. 2: w/ Rhy. Fig. 1 (2 times)

E7#9   E7   E7#9

way. _

Gtr. 3

steady gliss   steady gliss   steady gliss   grad. bend

Gtr. 1

let ring - - - - - ┤   let ring - - - - ┤   let ring - - - ┤   let ring - - - - - - ┤

Guitar Solo

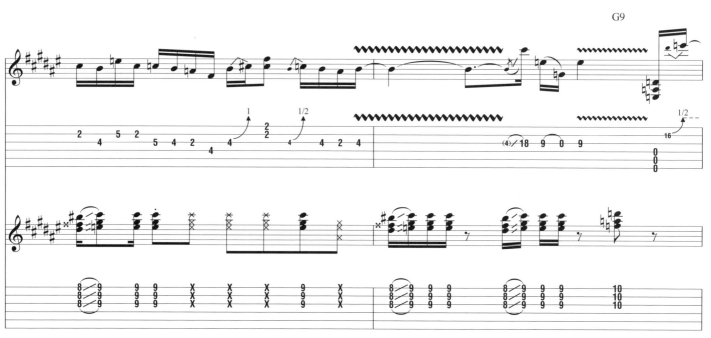

*Thumb lightly touches string at 7th fret producing harmonic.

F#9

D.S. al Coda

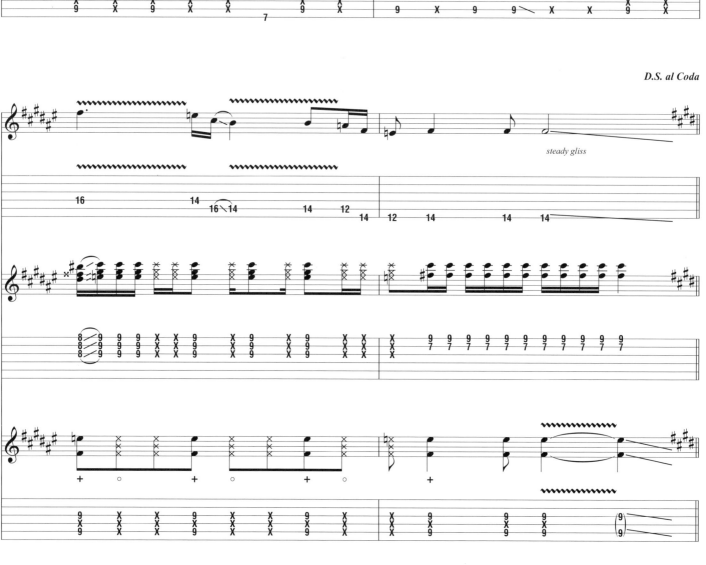

⊕ Coda

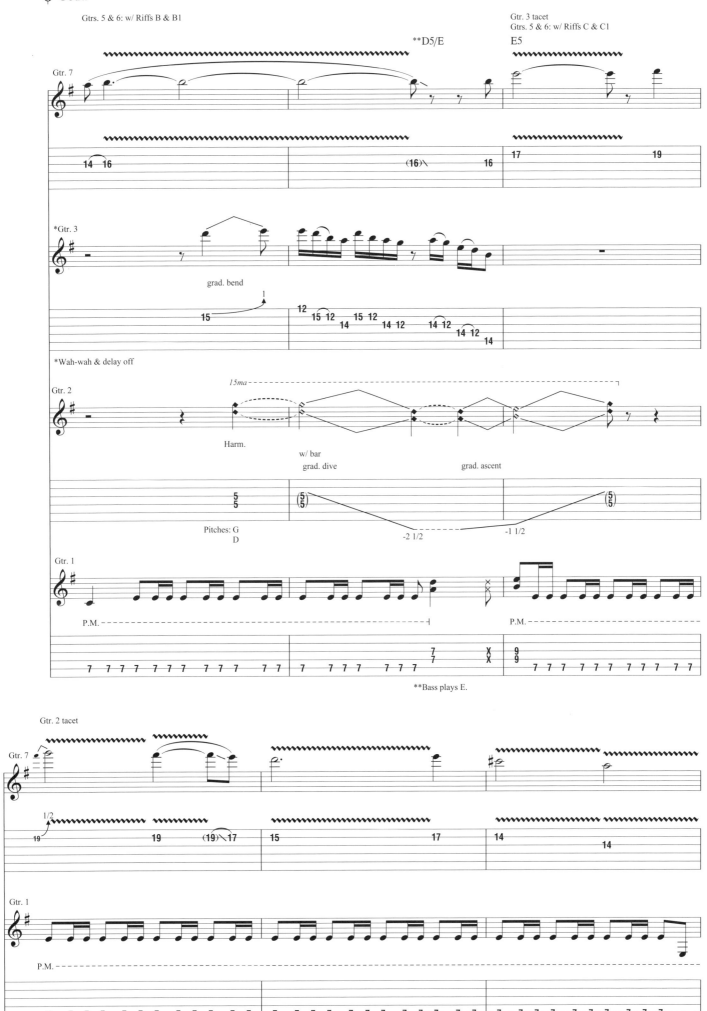

Interlude

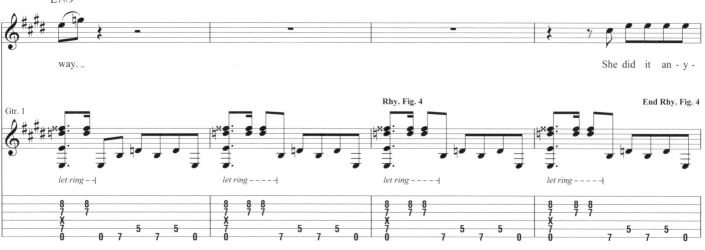

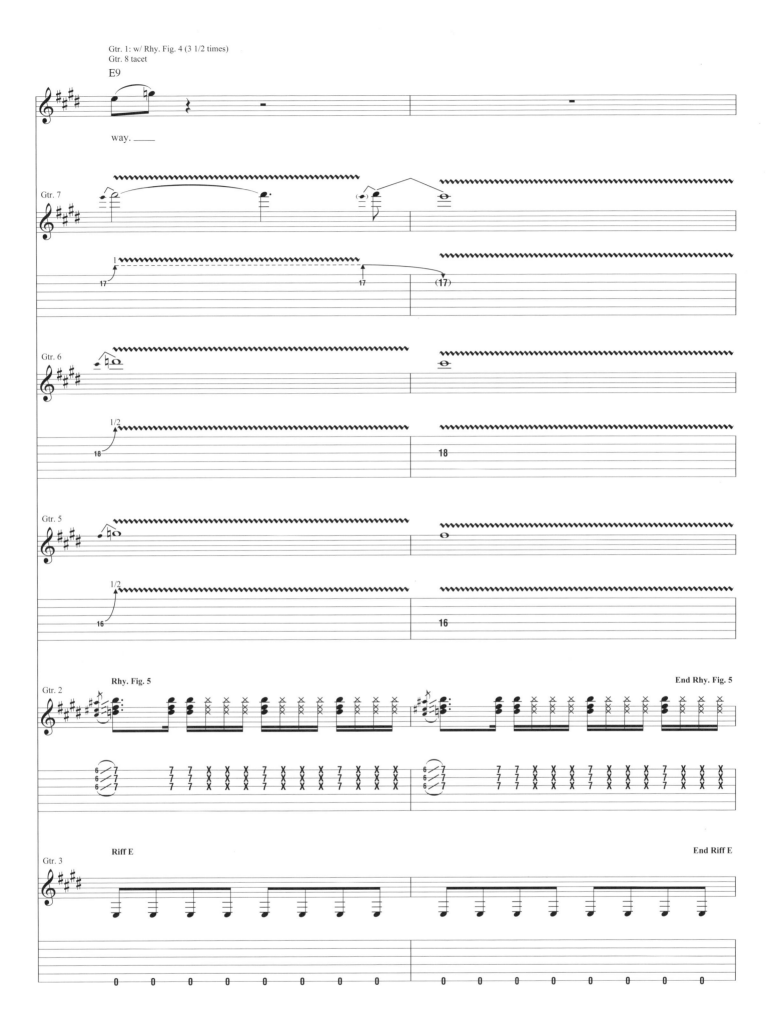

94

Beyond the Silence

Words and Music by Joe Bonamassa

Gtr. 1 (baritone gtr.) tuning:
(low to high) A-D-G-C-E-A

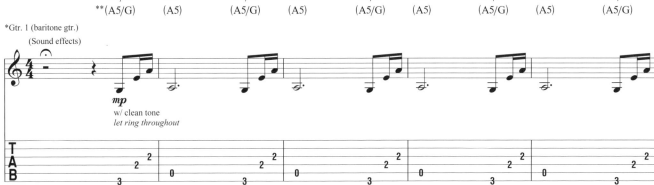

*Two baritone gtrs. arr. for one

**Symbols in parentheses represent chord names respective to baritone guitar.
Symbols above reflect actual sounding chords. To play this part on a standard guitar, capo V.

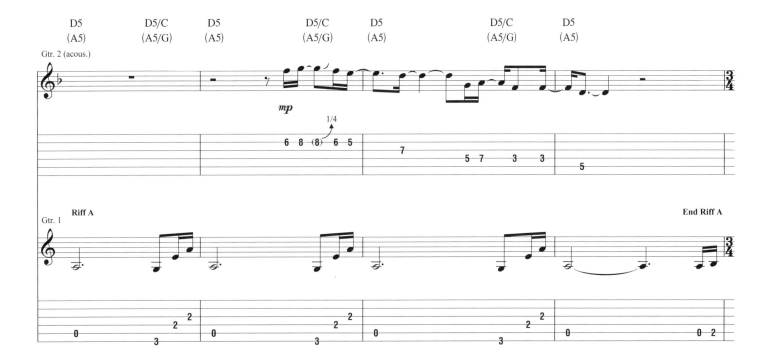

Lonely Boy

Words and Music by Joe Bonamassa, Jools Holland and Dave Stewart

*Chord symbols reflect implied harmony.

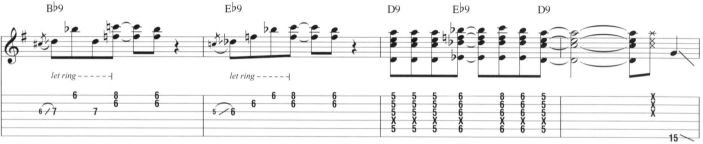

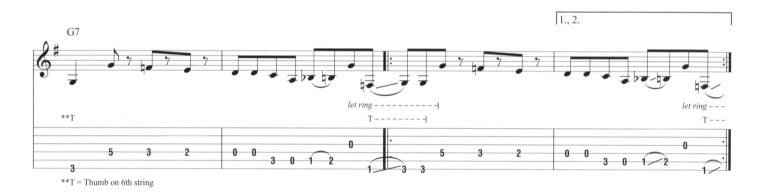

**T = Thumb on 6th string

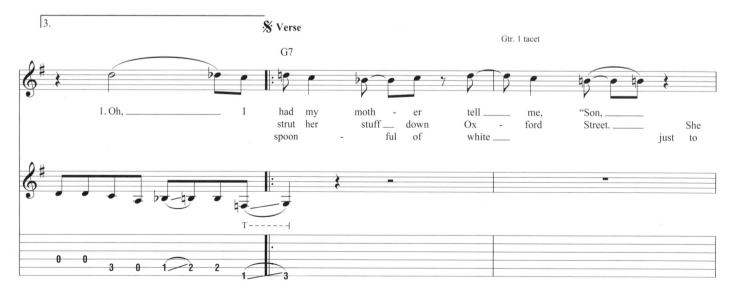

you have broth - ers but you're on - ly one." _____ She _____ knew _____ what _____ she
look - ing like _____ she had - n't eat. _____ I tell my - self, "What could _____
try to get her black. _____ I know my ba - by's gone. _____

had to do. _____ All my life _____ reach - ing out for you. I be -
_____ go wrong?" _____ An - oth - er tale _____ of the same old song. _____ I be -
She makes me blow _____ my stack. _____ I be -

Chorus
G7

lieve, _____ lone - ly boy this _____ time,

2nd time, Gtr. 1: w/ Fill 1
3rd time, Gtr. 1: w/ Fill 2

D7#9#5

{ now I'm _ a - lone }
{ oh, _ I'm a - lone } on this mat -
{ yeah, I'm _ a - lone }

Gtr. 1

let ring -

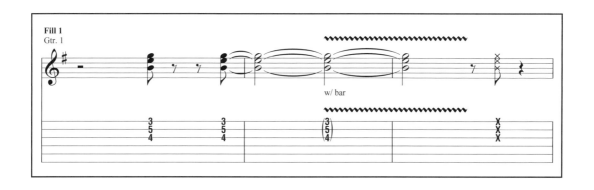

Fill 1
Gtr. 1

w/ bar

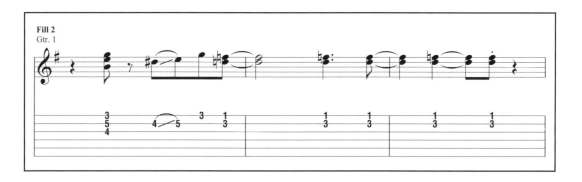

Fill 2
Gtr. 1

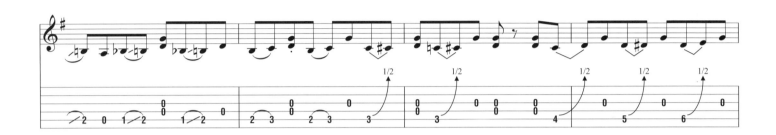

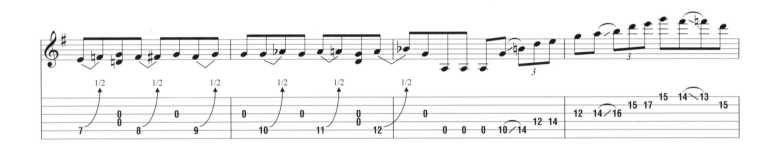

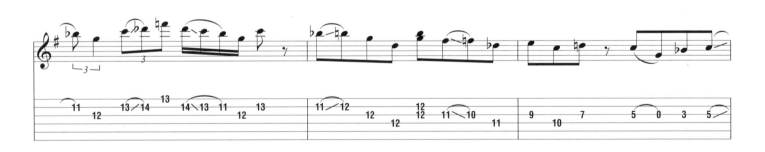

Verse

Gtr. 1 tacet

G7

- ly morn - ing, start - ing school; ___ soon be - came ___ the class - room fool. ___

Went to church ___ in my Sun - day shoes. ___ Peo - ple talk ___ a - bout my point of view, but I be -

Savannah

Words and Music by Joe Bonamassa and Bernie Marsden

Gtr. 4: Open A tuning:
(low to high) E-A-E-A-C#-E

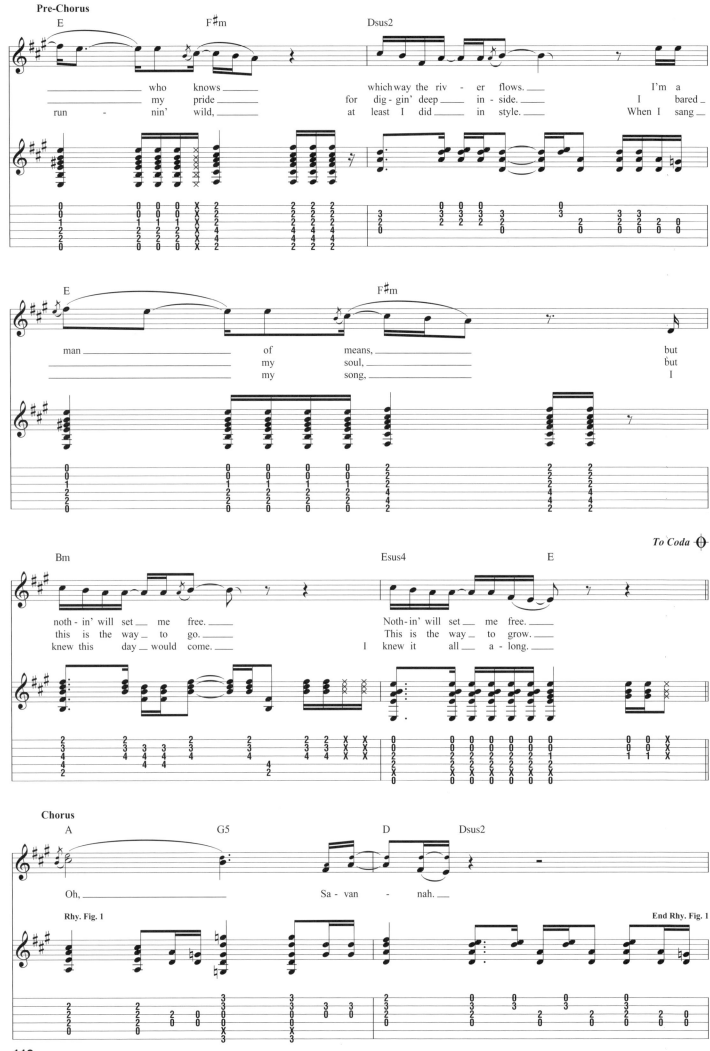

Interlude

Gtr. 1: w/ Riff A
Gtrs. 2 & 3: w/ Riff A1

Guitar Solo

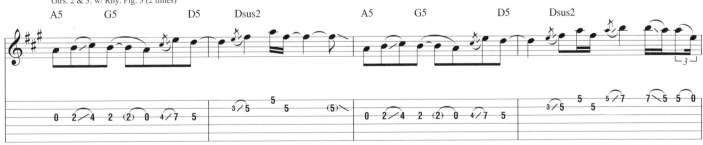

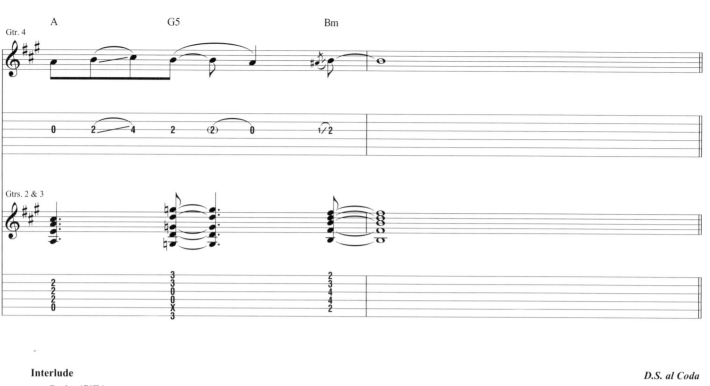

Interlude

Gtr. 1: w/ Riff A
Gtrs. 2 & 3: w/ Riff A1
Gtr. 4 tacet

D.S. al Coda

A

⊕ **Coda**

Chorus

Gtrs. 2 & 3: w/ Rhy. Fig. 1 (3 times)

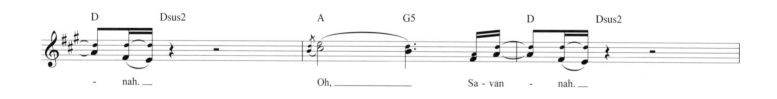

Oh, _____ Sa - van - nah. _____ Oh, _____ Sa - van -

- nah. _____ Oh, _____ Sa - van - nah. _____

Gtrs. 2 & 3: w/ Rhy. Fig. 2

Oh, _____ Sa - van - nah. You're more than home _____ to me. _____

Interlude

Gtr. 1: w/ Riff A
Gtrs. 2 & 3: w/ Riff A1

A

Outro-Guitar Solo

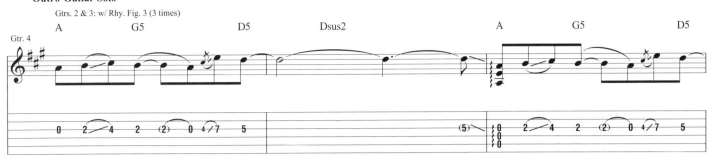

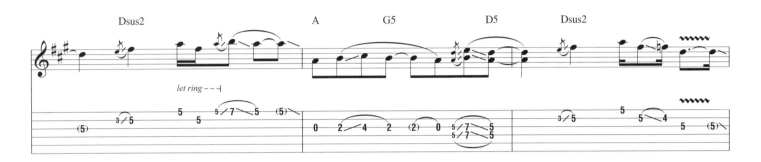

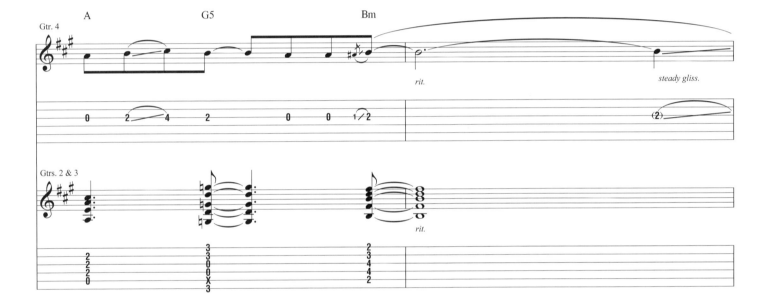

Free time

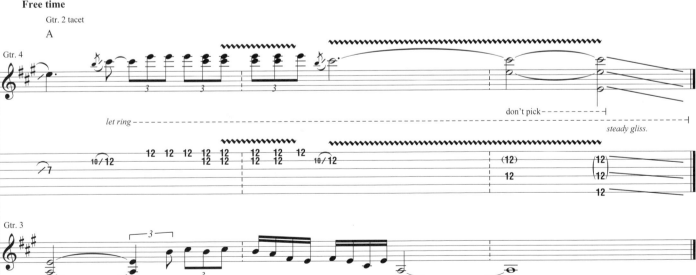

GUITAR NOTATION LEGEND

Guitar music can be notated three different ways: on a *musical staff*, in *tablature*, and in *rhythm slashes*.

RHYTHM SLASHES are written above the staff. Strum chords in the rhythm indicated. Use the chord diagrams found at the top of the first page of the transcription for the appropriate chord voicings. Round noteheads indicate single notes.

THE MUSICAL STAFF shows pitches and rhythms and is divided by bar lines into measures. Pitches are named after the first seven letters of the alphabet.

TABLATURE graphically represents the guitar fingerboard. Each horizontal line represents a string, and each number represents a fret.

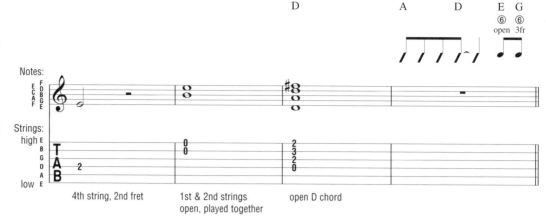

4th string, 2nd fret

1st & 2nd strings open, played together

open D chord

Definitions for Special Guitar Notation

HALF-STEP BEND: Strike the note and bend up 1/2 step.

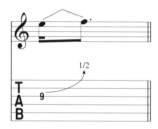

WHOLE-STEP BEND: Strike the note and bend up one step.

GRACE NOTE BEND: Strike the note and immediately bend up as indicated.

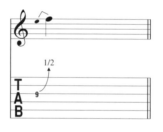

SLIGHT (MICROTONE) BEND: Strike the note and bend up 1/4 step.

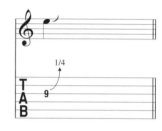

BEND AND RELEASE: Strike the note and bend up as indicated, then release back to the original note. Only the first note is struck.

PRE-BEND: Bend the note as indicated, then strike it.

PRE-BEND AND RELEASE: Bend the note as indicated. Strike it and release the bend back to the original note.

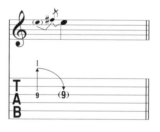

UNISON BEND: Strike the two notes simultaneously and bend the lower note up to the pitch of the higher.

VIBRATO: The string is vibrated by rapidly bending and releasing the note with the fretting hand.

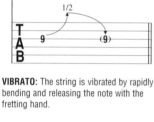

WIDE VIBRATO: The pitch is varied to a greater degree by vibrating with the fretting hand.

HAMMER-ON: Strike the first (lower) note with one finger, then sound the higher note (on the same string) with another finger by fretting it without picking.

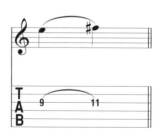

PULL-OFF: Place both fingers on the notes to be sounded. Strike the first note and without picking, pull the finger off to sound the second (lower) note.

LEGATO SLIDE: Strike the first note and then slide the same fret-hand finger up or down to the second note. The second note is not struck.

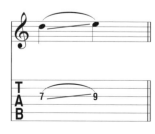

SHIFT SLIDE: Same as legato slide, except the second note is struck.

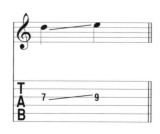

TRILL: Very rapidly alternate between the notes indicated by continuously hammering on and pulling off.

TAPPING: Hammer ("tap") the fret indicated with the pick-hand index or middle finger and pull off to the note fretted by the fret hand.

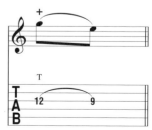

NATURAL HARMONIC: Strike the note while the fret-hand lightly touches the string directly over the fret indicated.

PINCH HARMONIC: The note is fretted normally and a harmonic is produced by adding the edge of the thumb or the tip of the index finger of the pick hand to the normal pick attack.

HARP HARMONIC: The note is fretted normally and a harmonic is produced by gently resting the pick hand's index finger directly above the indicated fret (in parentheses) while the pick hand's thumb or pick assists by plucking the appropriate string.

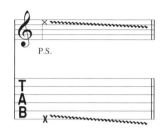

PICK SCRAPE: The edge of the pick is rubbed down (or up) the string, producing a scratchy sound.

MUFFLED STRINGS: A percussive sound is produced by laying the fret hand across the string(s) without depressing, and striking them with the pick hand.

PALM MUTING: The note is partially muted by the pick hand lightly touching the string(s) just before the bridge.

RAKE: Drag the pick across the strings indicated with a single motion.

TREMOLO PICKING: The note is picked as rapidly and continuously as possible.

ARPEGGIATE: Play the notes of the chord indicated by quickly rolling them from bottom to top.

VIBRATO BAR DIVE AND RETURN: The pitch of the note or chord is dropped a specified number of steps (in rhythm), then returned to the original pitch.

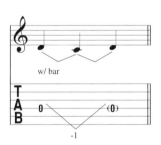

VIBRATO BAR SCOOP: Depress the bar just before striking the note, then quickly release the bar.

VIBRATO BAR DIP: Strike the note and then immediately drop a specified number of steps, then release back to the original pitch.

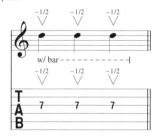

Additional Musical Definitions

(accent)	•	Accentuate note (play it louder).
(accent)	•	Accentuate note with great intensity.
(staccato)	•	Play the note short.
	•	Downstroke
∨	•	Upstroke

D.S. al Coda • Go back to the sign (%), then play until the measure marked "*To Coda*," then skip to the section labelled "**Coda**."

D.C. al Fine • Go back to the beginning of the song and play until the measure marked "*Fine*" (end).

Rhy. Fig. • Label used to recall a recurring accompaniment pattern (usually chordal).

Riff • Label used to recall composed, melodic lines (usually single notes) which recur.

Fill • Label used to identify a brief melodic figure which is to be inserted into the arrangement.

Rhy. Fill • A chordal version of a Fill.

tacet • Instrument is silent (drops out).

• Repeat measures between signs.

• When a repeated section has different endings, play the first ending only the first time and the second ending only the second time.

NOTE: Tablature numbers in parentheses mean:
1. The note is being sustained over a system (note in standard notation is tied), or
2. The note is sustained, but a new articulation (such as a hammer-on, pull-off, slide or vibrato) begins, or
3. The note is a barely audible "ghost" note (note in standard notation is also in parentheses).

GUITAR RECORDED VERSIONS®

AUTHENTIC TRANSCRIPTIONS WITH NOTES AND TABLATURE

Guitar Recorded Versions® are note-for-note transcriptions of guitar music taken directly off recordings. This series, one of the most popular in print today, features some of the greatest guitar players and groups from blues and rock to country and jazz.

Guitar Recorded Versions are transcribed by the best transcribers in the business. Every book contains notes and tablature unless otherwise marked. Visit **halleonard.com** for our complete selection.

Will Ackerman
00690016 The Will Ackerman Collection $22.99
Bryan Adams
00690501 Greatest Hits $24.99
Aerosmith
00690002 Big Ones $24.95
00690603 O Yeah! $27.99
Alice in Chains
00690178 Acoustic $19.99
00694865 Dirt $19.99
00660225 Facelift $19.99
00694925 Jar of Flies/Sap $19.99
00690387 Nothing Safe $24.99
All That Remains
00142819 The Order of Things $22.99
Allman Brothers Band
00694932 Definitive Collection, Volume 1 $27.99
00694933 Definitive Collection, Volume 2 $27.99
00694934 Definitive Collection, Volume 3 $29.99
Duane Allman
00690958 Guitar Anthology $29.99
Alter Bridge
00691071 AB III $29.99
00690945 Blackbird $24.99
00690755 One Day Remains $24.99
Anthrax
00690849 Best of Anthrax $19.99
Arctic Monkeys
00123558 AM $24.99
Chet Atkins
00690158 Almost Alone $22.99
00694876 Contemporary Styles $19.95
00694878 Vintage Fingerstyle $19.99
Audioslave
00690609 Audioslave $24.99
00690884 Revelations $19.95
Avenged Sevenfold
00690926 Avenged Sevenfold $24.99
00214869 Best of: 2005-2013 $24.99
00690820 City of Evil $24.95
00123216 Hail to the King $22.99
00691051 Nightmare $22.99
00222486 The Stage $24.99
00691065 Waking the Fallen $22.99
The Avett Brothers
00123140 Guitar Collection $22.99
Randy Bachman
00694918 Guitar Collection $22.95
The Beatles
00690489 1 (Number Ones) $24.99
00694929 1962-1966 $24.99
00694930 1967-1970 $27.99
00694880 Abbey Road $19.99
00694832 Acoustic Guitar $24.99
00691066 Beatles for Sale $22.99
00690903 Capitol Albums Vol. 2 $24.99
00691031 Help! $19.99
00690482 Let It Be $19.99
00691030 Magical Mystery Tour $22.99
00691067 Meet the Beatles! $22.99
00691068 Please Please Me $22.99
00694891 Revolver $19.99
00691014 Rock Band $34.99
00694914 Rubber Soul $22.99
00694863 Sgt. Pepper's Lonely Hearts Club Band $22.99
00110193 Tomorrow Never Knows $22.99
00690110 White Album Book 1 $19.99
00690111 White Album Book 2 $19.99
00690383 Yellow Submarine $19.95

The Beach Boys
00690503 Very Best $24.99
Beck
00690632 Beck – Sea Change $19.95
Jeff Beck
00691044 Best of Beck $24.99
00691042 Blow by Blow $22.99
00691041 Truth $19.99
00691043 Wired $19.99
George Benson
00694884 Best of $22.99
Chuck Berry
00692385 Chuck Berry $22.99
Billy Talent
00690835 Billy Talent $22.99
00690879 Billy Talent II $19.99
Black Crowes
00147787 Best of $19.99
The Black Keys
00129737 Turn Blue $22.99
Black Sabbath
00690149 Black Sabbath $17.99
00690901 Best of $22.99
00691010 Heaven and Hell $22.99
00690148 Master of Reality $19.99
00690142 Paranoid $17.99
00690145 Vol. 4 $22.99
00692200 We Sold Our Soul for Rock 'n' Roll $22.99
blink-182
00690389 Enema of the State $19.95
00690831 Greatest Hits $24.99
00691179 Neighborhoods $22.99
Michael Bloomfield
00148544 Guitar Anthology $24.99
Blue Öyster Cult
00690028 Cult Classics $19.99
Bon Jovi
00691074 Greatest Hits $24.99
Joe Bonamassa
00158600 Blues of Desperation $22.99
00139086 Different Shades of Blue $22.99
00198117 Muddy Wolf at Red Rocks $24.99
00283540 Redemption $24.99
Boston
00690913 Boston $19.99
00690932 Don't Look Back $19.99
00690829 Guitar Collection $24.99
David Bowie
00690491 Best of $19.99
Box Car Racer
00690583 Box Car Racer $19.95
Breaking Benjamin
00691023 Dear Agony $22.99
00690873 Phobia $19.99
Lenny Breau
00141446 Best of $19.99
Big Bill Broonzy
00286503 Guitar Collection $19.99
Roy Buchanan
00690168 Collection $24.99
Jeff Buckley
00690451 Collection $24.99
Bullet for My Valentine
00691047 Fever $22.99
00690957 Scream Aim Fire $22.99
00119629 Temper Temper $22.99
Kenny Burrell
00690678 Best of $22.99
Cage the Elephant
00691077 Thank You, Happy Birthday $22.99

The Cars
00691159 Complete Greatest Hits $22.99
Carter Family
00690261 Collection $19.99
Johnny Cash
00691079 Best of $22.99
Cheap Trick
00690043 Best of $19.95
Chicago
00690171 Definitive Guitar Collection $24.99
Chimaira
00691011 Guitar Collection $24.99
Charlie Christian
00690567 Definitive Collection $22.99
Eric Church
00101916 Chief $22.99
The Civil Wars
00129545 The Civil Wars $19.99
Eric Clapton
00690590 Anthology $34.99
00692391 Best of $22.95
00694896 Blues Breakers (with John Mayall) $19.99
00138731 The Breeze $22.99
00691055 Clapton $22.99
00690936 Complete Clapton $29.99
00690010 From the Cradle $22.99
00192383 I Still Do $19.99
00690363 Just One Night $24.99
00694873 Timepieces $19.95
00694869 Unplugged $24.99
00124873 Unplugged (Deluxe) $29.99
The Clash
00690162 Best of $19.99
Coheed & Cambria
00690828 IV $19.95
00139967 In Keeping Secrets of Silent Earth: 3 $24.99
Coldplay
00130786 Ghost Stories $19.99
00690593 A Rush of Blood to the Head $19.95
Collective Soul
00690855 Best of $19.95
Jessee Cook
00141704 Works Vol. 1 $19.99
Alice Cooper
00691091 Best of $24.99
Counting Crows
00694940 August & Everything After $19.99
Robert Cray
00127184 Best of $19.99
Cream
00694840 Disraeli Gears $24.99
Creed
00288787 Greatest Hits $22.99
Creedence Clearwater Revival
00690819 Best of $24.99
Jim Croce
00690648 The Very Best $19.99
Steve Cropper
00690572 Soul Man $22.99
Crosby, Stills & Nash
00690613 Best of $29.99
Cry of Love
00691171 Brother $22.99
Dick Dale
00690637 Best of $19.99
Daughtry
00690892 Daughtry $19.95
Alex de Grassi
00690822 Best of $19.95

Death Cab for Cutie
00690967 Narrow Stairs $22.99
Deep Purple
00690289 Best of $22.99
00690288 Machine Head $19.99
Def Leppard
00690784 Best of $24.99
Derek and the Dominos
00694831 Layla & Other Assorted Love Songs $24.99
Ani DiFranco
00690384 Best of $19.95
Dinosaur Jr.
00690979 Best of $22.99
The Doors
00690347 Anthology $22.95
00690348 Essential Collection $16.95
Dream Theater
00160579 The Astonishing $24.99
00122443 Dream Theater $24.99
00291164 Distance Over Time $24.99
Eagles
00278631 Their Greatest Hits 1971-1975 $22.99
00278632 Very Best of $34.99
Duane Eddy
00690250 Best of $19.99
Tommy Emmanuel
00147067 All I Want for Christmas $19.99
00690909 Best of $24.99
00172824 It's Never Too Late $22.99
00139220 Little by Little $24.99
Melissa Etheridge
00690555 Best of $19.95
Evanescence
00691186 Evanescence $22.99
Extreme
00690515 Pornograffitti $24.99
John Fahey
00150257 Guitar Anthology $19.99
Tal Farlow
00125661 Best of $19.99
Five Finger Death Punch
00691009 5 Finger Death Punch $19.99
00691181 American Capitalism $22.99
00128917 Wrong Side of Heaven & Righteous Side of Hell $22.99
Fleetwood Mac
00690664 Best of $24.99
Flyleaf
00690870 Flyleaf $19.95
Foghat
00690986 Best of $22.99
Foo Fighters
00691024 Greatest Hits $22.99
00691115 Wasting Light $22.99
Peter Frampton
00690842 Best of $22.99
Robben Ford
00690805 Best of $24.99
00120220 Guitar Anthology $29.99
Free
00694920 Best of $19.99
Rory Gallagher
00295410 Blues (Selections) $24.99
Danny Gatton
00694807 88 Elmira St $22.99
Genesis
00690438 Guitar Anthology $24.99
Godsmack
00120167 Godsmack $19.95
00691048 The Oracle $22.99
Goo Goo Dolls
00690943 Greatest Hits Vol. 1 $24.99

Grateful Dead
00139460 Guitar Anthology $29.99
Green Day
00212480 Revolution Radio $19.99
00118259 ¡Tré! $21.99
00113073 ¡Uno! $21.99
Peter Green
00691190 Best of $24.99
Greta Van Fleet
00287517 Anthem of the Peaceful Army $19.99
00287515 From the Fires $19.99
Patty Griffin
00690927 Children Running Through $19.95
Guns N' Roses
00690978 Chinese Democracy $24.99
Buddy Guy
00691027 Anthology $24.99
00694854 Damn Right, I've Got the Blues $19.95
Jim Hall
00690697 Best of $19.99
Ben Harper
00690840 Both Sides of the Gun $19.95
00691018 Fight for Your Mind $22.99
George Harrison
00694798 Anthology $22.99
Scott Henderson
00690841 Blues Guitar Collection $24.99
Jimi Hendrix
00692930 Are You Experienced? $27.99
00692931 Axis: Bold As Love $24.99
00690304 Band of Gypsys $24.99
00690608 Blue Wild Angel $24.95
00275044 Both Sides of the Sky $22.99
00692932 Electric Ladyland $27.99
00690017 Live at Woodstock $29.99
00119619 People, Hell & Angels $24.99
00690602 Smash Hits $24.99
00691152 West Coast Seattle Boy (Anthology) $29.99
00691332 Winterland $22.99
H.I.M.
00690843 Dark Light $19.95
Buddy Holly
00660029 Best of $22.99
John Lee Hooker
00690793 Anthology $29.99
Howlin' Wolf
00694905 Howlin' Wolf $22.99
Billy Idol
00690692 Very Best of $22.99
Imagine Dragons
00121961 Night Visions $22.99
Incubus
00690688 A Crow Left of the Murder $19.95
Iron Maiden
00690790 Anthology $24.99
00691058 The Final Frontier $22.99
00200446 Guitar Tab $29.99
00690887 A Matter of Life and Death $24.95
Alan Jackson
00690730 Guitar Collection $29.99
Elmore James
00696938 Master of the Electric Slide Guitar $19.99
Jane's Addiction
00690652 Best of $19.95
Jethro Tull
00690684 Aqualung $22.99
00690693 Guitar Anthology $24.99
00691182 Stand Up $22.99

John 5
00690898 The Devil Knows My Name...$22.95
00690814 Songs for Sanity...$19.95
00690751 Vertigo...$19.95

Eric Johnson
00694912 Ah Via Musicom...$24.99
00690660 Best of...$27.99
00691076 Up Close...$22.99
00690169 Venus Isle...$27.99

Jack Johnson
00690846 Curious George...$19.95

Robert Johnson
00690271 New Transcriptions...$24.99

Janis Joplin
00699131 Best of...$19.95

Judas Priest
00690427 Best of...$24.99

Kansas
00690277 Best of...$19.99

Phil Keaggy
00690911 Best of...$24.99

Toby Keith
00690727 Guitar Collection...$19.99

The Killers
00690910 Sam's Town...$19.95

Killswitch Engage
00120814 Disarm the Descent...$22.99

Albert King
00690504 Very Best of...$24.99
00124869 In Session...$22.99

B.B. King
00690492 Anthology...$24.99
00130447 Live at the Regal...$17.99
00690444 Riding with the King..$24.99

Freddie King
00690134 Collection...$19.99

Marcus King
00327968 El Dorado...$22.99

Kiss
00690157 Alive!...$19.99
00690356 Alive II...$22.99
00694903 Best of...$24.99
00690355 Destroyer...$17.99
00291163 Very Best of...$24.99

Mark Knopfler
00690164 Guitar Styles...$24.99

Korn
00690780 Greatest Hits Vol. 1...$24.99

Kris Kristofferson
00690377 Collection...$19.99

Lamb of God
00690834 Ashes of the Wake...$24.99
00691187 Resolution...$22.99
00690875 Sacrament...$22.99

Ray LaMontagne
00690977 Gossip in the Grain...$19.99
00691057 God Willin' & The Creek Don't Rise...$22.99
00690890 Til the Sun Turns Black$19.95

Jonny Lang
00690658 Long Time Coming...$19.95

John Lennon
00690679 Guitar Collection...$24.99

Linkin Park
00690922 Minutes to Midnight..$19.99

Los Lonely Boys
00690743 Los Lonely Boys...$19.95

The Lumineers
00114563 The Lumineers...$22.99

George Lynch
00690525 Best of...$24.99

Lynyrd Skynyrd
00690955 All-Time Greatest Hits.$24.99
00694954 New Best of...$24.99

Yngwie Malmsteen
00690577 Anthology...$29.99

Marilyn Manson
00690754 Lest We Forget...$19.95

Bob Marley
00694956 Legend...$19.99
00694945 Songs of Freedom...$29.99

Maroon 5
00690657 Songs About Jane...$19.95

Pat Martino
00139168 Guitar Anthology...$24.99

John McLaughlin
00129105 Guitar Tab Anthology...$24.99

Mastodon
00690989 Crack the Skye...$24.99
00236690 Emperor of Sand...$22.99
00691176 The Hunter...$22.99
00137718 Once More 'Round the Sun...$22.99

Andy McKee
00691942 Art of Motion...$24.99
00691034 Joyland...$19.99

Don McLean
00120080 Songbook...$19.99

Megadeth
00690481 Capitol Punishment...$22.99
00694952 Countdown to Extinction...$24.99
00691015 Endgame...$24.99
00276065 Greatest Hits...$24.99
00694951 Rust in Peace...$24.99
00691185 Th1rt3en...$22.99
00690011 Youthanasia...$24.99

John Mellencamp
00690505 Guitar Collection...$24.99

Metallica
00209876 Hardwired... To Self-Destruct...$22.99

Pat Metheny
00690562 Bright Size Life...$24.99
00691073 Day Trip/ Tokyo Day Trip Live...$22.99
00690646 One Quiet Night...$24.99
00690559 Question & Answer...$24.99
00690565 Rejoicing...$19.95
00690558 Trio 99-00...$24.99
00690561 Trio Live...$22.95
00118836 Unity Band...$22.99
00102590 What's It All About...$24.99

Steve Miller Band
00690040 Young Hearts: Complete Greatest Hits...$24.99

Ministry
00119338 Guitar Tab Collection ..$24.99

Wes Montgomery
00102591 Guitar Anthology...$24.99

Gary Moore
00691092 Best of...$24.99
00694802 Still Got the Blues...$24.99

Alanis Morissette
00355456 Jagged Little Pill...$22.99

Motion City Soundtrack
00691005 Best of...$19.99

Mountain
00694958 Best of...$19.99

Mudvayne
00690794 Lost and Found...$19.95

Mumford & Sons
00691070 Sigh No More...$22.99

Muse
00118196 The 2nd Law...$19.99
00151195 Drones...$19.99

My Morning Jacket
00690996 Collection...$19.99

Matt Nathanson
00690984 Some Mad Hope...$22.99

Night Ranger
00690883 Best of...$19.99

Nirvana
00690611 Nirvana...$22.95
00694895 Bleach...$19.99
00694913 In Utero...$19.99
00694883 Nevermind...$19.99
00690026 Unplugged in New York $19.99

No Doubt
00120112 Tragic Kingdom...$22.95

Nothing More
00265439 Guitar & Bass Tab Collection...$24.99

The Offspring
00690807 Greatest Hits...$22.99

Opeth
00243349 Best of...$22.99

Roy Orbison
00691052 Black & White Night..$22.99

Ozzy Osbourne
00694847 Best of...$24.99

Brad Paisley
00690933 Best of...$27.99
00690995 Play...$24.99

Christopher Parkening
00690938 Duets & Concertos...$24.99
00690939 Solo Pieces...$19.99

Les Paul
00690594 Best of...$22.99

Pearl Jam
00694855 Ten...$22.99

Periphery
00146043 Guitar Tab Collection..$24.99

Carl Perkins
00690725 Best of...$19.99

Tom Petty
00690499 Definitive Collection ..$22.99

Phish
00690176 Billy Breathes...$24.99

Pink Floyd
00121933 Acoustic Collection...$24.99
00690428 Dark Side of the Moon$19.99
00142677 The Endless River...$19.99
00244637 Guitar Anthology...$24.99
00239799 The Wall...$24.99

Poison
00690789 Best of...$19.99

Elvis Presley
00692535 Elvis Presley...$19.95
00690299 King of Rock 'n' Roll.$22.99

Prince
00690925 Very Best of...$24.99

Queen
00690003 Classic Queen...$24.99
00694975 Greatest Hits...$25.99

Queens of the Stone Age
00254332 Villains...$22.99

Queensryche
00690670 Very Best of...$24.99

The Raconteurs
00690878 Broken Boy Soldiers...$19.95

Radiohead
00109303 Guitar Anthology...$24.99

Rage Against the Machine
00694910 Rage Against the Machine...$22.99
00119834 Guitar Anthology...$24.99

Rancid
00690179 And Out Come the Wolves...$24.99

Ratt
00690426 Best of...$19.95

Red Hot Chili Peppers
00690055 BloodSugarSexMagik..$19.99
00690584 By the Way...$24.99
00690379 Californication...$19.99
00182634 The Getaway...$24.99
00690673 Greatest Hits...$22.99
00691166 I'm with You...$22.99
00690255 Mother's Milk...$19.95
00690090 One Hot Minute...$22.95
00690852 Stadium Arcadium...$29.99

The Red Jumpsuit Apparatus
00690893 Don't You Fake It...$19.95

Jerry Reed
00694892 Guitar Style of...$22.99

Django Reinhardt
00690511 Definitive Collection ..$24.99

Jimmie Rodgers
00690260 Guitar Collection...$22.99

Rolling Stones
00690014 Exile on Main Street..$24.99
00690631 Guitar Anthology...$29.99
00690186 Rock and Roll Circus.$19.95
00694976 Some Girls...$22.95
00690264 Tattoo You...$19.95

Angelo Romero
00690974 Bella...$19.99

David Lee Roth
00690685 Eat 'Em and Smile...$22.99
00690694 Guitar Anthology...$24.95
00690942 Songs of Van Halen...$19.95

Rush
00323854 The Spirit of Radio...$22.99

Santana
00173534 Guitar Anthology...$27.99
00690031 Greatest Hits...$19.95

Joe Satriani
00276350 What Happens Next ..$24.99

Michael Schenker
00690796 Very Best of...$24.99

Matt Schofield
00128870 Guitar Tab Collection ..$22.99

Scorpions
00690566 Best of...$24.99

Bob Seger
00690659 Greatest Hits Vol. 2...$17.95
00690604 Guitar Collection...$22.99

Ed Sheeran
00234543 Divide...$19.99
00138870 X...$19.99

Kenny Wayne Shepherd
00690803 Best of...$24.99
00151178 Ledbetter Heights...$19.99

Shinedown
00692433 Amaryllis...$22.99

Silverchair
00690196 Freak Show...$19.99

Skillet
00122218 Rise...$22.99

Slash
00691114 Guitar Anthology...$29.99

Slayer
00690872 Christ Illusion...$19.95
00690813 Guitar Collection...$19.99

Slipknot
00690419 Slipknot...$19.99
00690973 All Hope Is Gone...$24.99

Smashing Pumpkins
00316982 Greatest Hits...$22.99

Social Distortion
00690330 Live at the Roxy...$22.99

Soundgarden
00690912 Guitar Anthology...$24.99

Steely Dan
00120004 Best of...$24.99

Steppenwolf
00694921 Best of...$22.95

Mike Stern
00690655 Best of...$24.99

Cat Stevens
14041588 Tea for the Tillerman..$19.99

Rod Stewart
00690949 Guitar Anthology...$19.99

Stone Sour
00690877 Come What(ever) May $19.95

Styx
00690520 Guitar Collection...$22.99

Sublime
00120081 Sublime...$19.99
00120122 40 oz. to Freedom...$22.99
00690992 Robbin' the Hood...$19.99

SUM 41
00690519 All Killer No Filler...$19.95
00690929 Underclass Hero...$19.95

Supertramp
00691072 Best of...$24.99

Taylor Swift
00690994 Taylor Swift...$22.99
00690993 Fearless...$22.99
00115957 Red...$21.99
00691063 Speak Now...$22.99

System of a Down
00690531 Toxicity...$19.99

James Taylor
00694824 Best of...$19.99

Thin Lizzy
00694887 Best of...$19.99

.38 Special
00690988 Guitar Anthology...$22.99

Three Days Grace
00691039 Life Starts Now...$22.99

Trans-Siberian Orchestra
00150209 Guitar Anthology...$19.99

Merle Travis
00690233 Collection...$22.99

Trivium
00253237 Guitar Tab Anthology...$24.99
00123862 Vengeance Falls...$22.99

Robin Trower
00690683 Bridge of Sighs...$19.99

U2
00699191 Best of: 1980-1990 ...$24.99
00690732 Best of: 1990-2000 ...$24.99
00690894 18 Singles...$22.99

Keith Urban
00124461 Guitar Anthology...$19.99

Steve Vai
00690039 Alien Love Secrets...$24.99
00690575 Alive in an Ultra World$22.95
00690172 Fire Garden...$24.95
00690343 Flex-Able Leftovers...$19.95
00156024 Guitar Anthology...$34.99
00197570 Modern Primitive...$29.99
00660137 Passion & Warfare...$27.50
00690881 Real Illusions: Reflections...$27.99
00690605 The Elusive Light and Sound, Vol. 1...$29.99
00694904 Sex and Religion...$24.95
00110385 The Story of Light...$24.99
00690392 The Ultra Zone...$19.95

Van Halen
00700555 Van Halen...$19.99
00295076 30 Classics...$29.99
00700092 1984...$24.99
00700558 Fair Warning...$22.99

Jimmie Vaughan
00690690 Best of...$19.95

Stevie Ray Vaughan
00690024 Couldn't Stand the Weather...$19.99
00690116 Guitar Collection...$24.95
00694879 In the Beginning...$19.95
00660136 In Step...$22.99
00660058 Lightnin' Blues 83-87.$29.99
00690550 Live at Montreux...$27.99
00217455 Plays Slow Blues...$19.99
00694835 The Sky Is Crying...$24.99
00690025 Soul to Soul...$19.95
00690015 Texas Flood...$19.99

Volbeat
00109770 Guitar Collection...$22.99
00121808 Outlaw Gentlemen & Shady Ladies...$22.99

T-Bone Walker
00690132 Collection...$19.99

Muddy Waters
00694789 Deep Blues...$24.99

Doc Watson
00152161 Guitar Anthology...$22.99

Weezer
00690071 The Blue Album...$19.99
00691046 Rarities Edition...$22.99

Paul Westerberg & The Replacements
00691036 Very Best of...$19.99

Whitesnake
00117511 Guitar Collection...$24.99

The Who
00691941 Acoustic Guitar Collection...$22.99
00690447 Best of...$24.99

Wilco
00691006 Guitar Collection...$22.99

Stevie Wonder
00690319 Hits...$22.99

The Yardbirds
00690596 Best of...$22.99

Yes
00122303 Guitar Collection...$22.99

Dwight Yoakam
00690916 Best of...$19.95

Frank Zappa
00690507 Apostrophe...$22.99
00690443 Hot Rats...$22.99
00690624 One Size Fits All...$27.99
00690623 Over-Nite Sensation ..$24.99

ZZ Top
00121684 Early Classics...$27.99
00690589 Guitar Anthology...$24.99
00690960 Guitar Classics...$19.99